ESSAYS ON BOOKS

ESSAYS ON BOOKS

BY

A. CLUTTON-BROCK

Essay Index Reprint Series

91947

BOOKS FOR LIBRARIES PRESS
FREEPORT, NEW YORK

First Published 1920
Reprinted 1968

LIBRARY OF CONGRESS CATALOG CARD NUMBER:
68-29198

PRINTED IN THE UNITED STATES OF AMERICA

PREFACE

THESE Essays are all reprinted from the Literary Supplement of *The Times*, with a few corrections and a few passages left out. Some of the essays were written on particular occasions, the death of a writer or the anniversary of his birth or death. These consist chiefly of praise, but I was glad of the chance to praise great men, especially Swinburne, who is now suspected by the old and neglected by the young. The essay on Shakespeare was a task set me; yet I enjoyed writing it when forced to do so. The essays on the Brontës and on Turgenev were provoked by books with which, in spite of their merits, I disagreed more than I agreed. I reprint them because the opinions I oppose in them are, I think, common.

A. CLUTTON-BROCK

GODALMING
October 1920

CONTENTS

ESSAYS ON BOOKS

Shakespeare ❧ ❧ ❧ ❧ ❧

(Written for the Tercentenary of his death)

WE know little about Shakespeare, yet
we may be sure that he would be
surprised rather than pleased to find that he
had become an institution. If I must be an
institution—we can fancy him saying—let it
be called Bacon rather than Shakespeare. But
the desire to call the institutional Shakespeare
Bacon is inevitable; for, if all these plays are
perfect, if they always manifest omniscience,
omnipotence, and the loftiest intentions, they
must have been produced by a god; and we do
know enough about Shakespeare to be sure
that he was not like a god. We know that he
was something of a hack, like Mozart and
Tintoret; he wrote to earn his living, and
did not care much what became of his plays
after they had been acted. He never even had
a university education, and there are one or

A   I

two scandalous stories about him. How could such a man become an institution? One could not imagine him even a Trustee of the British Museum, like the Archbishop of Canterbury or the Lord Chancellor. These are the men fit to become institutions—and there was a contemporary Lord Chancellor capable of anything, a universal genius. Not an artist, perhaps, but Shakespeare's plays have ceased to be works of art since they became perfect; we do not enjoy them so much as the sense that we are doing our duty to our King and Country when we read them or see them—well, not acted, but presented.

If Shakespeare could see them acted now he would know how unworthy he was to have written them. For this kind of performance, he would say, I should have written something quite different; and if he could read some of the books about him, he would say—For this kind of criticism I ought to have written something no less different. In fact, he would not know himself at all in that institution whose tercentenary we are now celebrating, and he might wish that we should celebrate it by abolishing it. For artists have their peculiar vanities, and one of them is a desire to be liked for what they have done best. The real

Shakespeare

Shakespeare must have known quite well that, like other human beings, he did not always do his best; but this institutional Shakespeare always did his best, and therefore he is not a human being and so not an artist. He is praised indiscriminately for passages of which the real Shakespeare must have been a little ashamed, if he ever remembered them, and of which he would certainly not care to be reminded; and the effect of this praise is to make him seem almost a dull writer. But the real Shakespeare, unlike some of the greatest poets, was at great pains not to be dull; he was an entertainer who succeeded because he was himself much entertained with life ; he could be amused even by bores, and so he could make them amusing. But the bores have had their posthumous revenge upon him ; they have almost persuaded us that he is too great and good to be amusing, and they have made a practice of quoting in speeches and books those passages from him which are least amusing, which, divorced from their context, seem almost dull.

As an artist Shakespeare has been more sinned against than sinning, and yet he certainly sinned. He wrote from hand to mouth, and was often content with his second best both in conception and in execution. We may guess that he had an itch for writing, which was encouraged by his enormous professional facility. No doubt he enjoyed his own rhetoric, enjoyed writing it and hearing it spouted on the stage; but he would not have enjoyed hearing a bore quote it as if it were gospel. He knew well enough that his rhetoric was only a useful makeshift, even if he had the Elizabethan love of it. At that time rhetoric was a new weapon, as sweeping gestures were to the painters of the Cinquecento. The Elizabethan felt that he owed some rhetoric to his audience, and when he wished to ease their minds from the strain of rapid events he turned it on as a modern playwright might turn on epigram. The actors declaimed it swiftly and the audience liked it, as we like the arpeggios of a virtuoso pianist; yet it was not meant to be listened to very closely. But now, with our modern habit of reading Shakespeare rather than acting him, we do listen to Shakespeare's rhetoric closely, and pedants tell us that it is all high poetry. What is more, actors declaim it as if it were the funeral oration of Pericles, and so slowly that they are forced to cut Shakespeare's best to make room for it. So there are some who are

tempted to revolt against him as a mere
rhetorician.

He was a great rhetorician, but not
because he trusted in rhetoric. Among the
chief poets of the world there is none who can
let himself go so completely as Shakespeare,
none who can surrender himself so utterly to a
conception and to an execution worthy of it.
But he needed to practise this power of surrender both in his conception and in his execution. We may guess that, provided he made
himself capable of the highest, he did not care
much if he often fell below it in the process.
He was not a sublime egotist and he had no
egotistical love of perfection. What he desired was to be equal to the Heaven-sent
moment when it came; and he never knew
when it would come in the course of his trade.
He was cleverer even than Fletcher—no one
ever was so clever as Shakespeare—but his
cleverness was tolerable to him only because
he could rise through it when the Heaven-sent
moment came. Worldlings make the best
saints, and Shakespeare is the worldling among
all the great saints of poetry. Much nonsense
has been talked about his omniscience, but he
did know more about the art of literature than
any other poet, because he practised more of

it; and he alone of all the greatest poets of the world was able to enrich his masterpieces with the whole art of literature. *Hamlet* is a masterpiece like the *Divine Comedy* or the *Iliad* or the *Agamemnon*, but how much more amusing it is than any of those works. The Prince of Denmark is a figure of high poetry like Milton's Prince of Darkness, yet we know him as well as Peter in *War and Peace*, while Polonius and Osric are as near to us as anyone in Dickens. In the Fool in *King Lear* Dickens and Æschylus are, as it were, fused, and in Cordelia, Sophocles and Dostoevsky. For Cordelia is something of a shrew; we can project her into the modern home as we could not project Antigone. We can see her in the clothes of to-day; we could marry her even and be a little afraid of her fierceness or lovingly amused by it. These are all figures that could be translated without incongruity into comedy; for Shakespeare lived in that world, too, lived and moved and had his being in it. He rose out of prose into poetry as naturally as Mozart rose into melody. He was a professional writer, but not a professional poet like Milton or Dante; he practised no austerities of art or of experience, but opened his mind to earth and heaven,

living and writing as if he were just an ordinary
man with a gift.

We say *living*, because in spite of the little
that is known about him we know that his
art must express the life of his mind. He
must have lived more largely than Dante or
Milton, must have wasted his time more, have
been less fastidious with himself and with
others. Of all the great poets, he is the
most at ease with prose and with the prose
way of thinking. The difference between
prose and poetry in works of imagination
is mainly in speed of thought; and Shakespeare could think fast or slow as the mood
took him; he could linger like an epicure
over the character of men and things even
when they were ugly or absurd, where Milton
would have rushed past them in angry im-
patience. It was indeed the peculiar power
of his imagination to conceive a tragedy in
relation to the whole diverse, incoherent world
of reality, and to preserve the diversity, the
incoherence, the inattention of it all, even at
the tragic height. There are other tragedies
as intense as *King Lear*, but there is none of
equal intensity so rich in content, none so
closely connected with the world as we know
it, none so full of characters that we should

recognize if we met them. And because the
characters are thus fully drawn, the tragic
conflict between them is sharper than it ever
is between the noble shadows of the Greek
drama. There is a struggle of actual flesh
and blood; there are secrets revealed about
ourselves, as in Dostoevsky; but it is Dostoevsky
set to music and with ten times the power of
expression that any novelist ever had. The
novelist can tell us about his characters'
emotions, but Shakespeare can make their
emotions as strong to us as to themselves.
He can put into words, not merely the subtlety,
but also the force, of states of the soul; he
has the science of the psychologist and the
music of the poet combined as no one has
combined them before or since.

This combination is his peculiar excellence;
and his form is made to suit it. We never
see that form in his plays as they are commonly
acted now, nor can we be fully aware of it
when we read them. For his method is, as it
were, to assume a rushing current of events
and to throw a searchlight upon different
points in that current. In the Greek drama
the convention is that all the action is presented
on the stage except what is related. The
audience knows all the facts from first to last,

and the facts are carefully selected so that they may all be known. Shakespeare's way is rather to give us swift glimpses of the whole actual complexity of life; and his art is to choose them so that we see the connexion between one glimpse and another, so that they have a cumulative power upon us. But he does not aim at continuity, and to force any kind of continuity upon him, as is commonly done in modern versions of his plays, is to spoil his form. He set out to be a dramatist; and we cannot see his dramatic greatness, the excellence of his construction, or the power which made his method possible, if his plays are robbed of their form. For he has the peculiar power of making his characters come to life and be themselves the moment they appear on the stage. Hamlet is Hamlet in the first words he speaks. Language identifies him as people in real life are identified by their faces; yet at the same time it is used to carry on the action of the play, and things happen as swiftly as in a play of mere situation. But when Hamlet soliloquizes, it is not merely an outworn dramatic device; for his thoughts are so phrased that we recognize his mind as if it were a well-known face. And this power of giving instant life to a character is what gives life also to Shakespeare's form; for, without it, there would be no continuity in the glimpses of his searchlight. It is the characters themselves, the moment they appear, that connect one glimpse with another and convince us that they are glimpses of a real world which continues in all its complexity and richness between the glimpses. Hamlet, Cordelia, Othello, Macbeth, Iago, seem to have a life independent of the play. We feel that we see only a little of them and can deduce much more. We are aware of their existence between the scenes in which they appear; for, when they enter, they are already absorbed in their business, and, when they depart, they are still absorbed in it. That is where Shakespeare differs from Ibsen, whose characters live only in their dramatic relation with each other. We cannot think of them apart from the play, for he seems to create them only for dramatic purposes and to care for them only dramatically. They are puppets into which he breathes life; and when the curtain falls they are put back into the cupboard. But Shakespeare seems to throw his searchlight upon living men and women, to control the light and not the characters. And he seems to love them, too, as if they had been made by God, not by

himself; the world of his plays is not a world
of his contrivance. In that he is like the
greatest painters, who seem not to compose
their pictures but merely to lay the emphasis
of their own delight on what they have seen.
There are people who will tell you that in
construction Shakespeare is a fool to Ibsen;
but he was playing a different game and one
more difficult. He cannot do as he will with
his characters to make a play, because they are
not his characters; they have come to life in
his mind, and he can only choose his glimpses
of them. But the wonder is that in this
independent life of theirs they still speak with
his power of words and yet out of their own
minds and in their own character. Hamlet
has all Shakespeare's genius of expression; he
talks as Shakespeare himself could talk only
in the ecstasy of creation; yet it is always
Hamlet who talks, and not a poet at large.
And even at those moments when the theme
of the play passes, as it were, into pure music,
when the action fades away and we see only a
naked soul before us utterly aware of itself and
its relation to the universe, it is still the soul
of Hamlet or King Lear that speaks or thinks,
and not the mere comment of the poet. He
is always the dramatist, even when his drama

rises above all circumstance of time or place;
when his characters have forgotten the world,
he does not forget them.

And because his characters thus come to
life in his mind he is equal master of tragedy
and comedy, which are both part of the real
life of man and in a living man cannot be
separated for dramatic purposes. Hamlet,
Macbeth, King Lear are too real to be dignified
always; they forget themselves and forget that
they are tragic figures. The world in which
they live is not purely tragic, for it is the real
world, although Shakespeare may give us
mainly tragic glimpses of it. And so Falstaff
is not purely comic. He possessed Shakespeare's mind and took on an independent life
of his own; he was the first figure that
Shakespeare created with the whole of his
power, and so the first that does not seem to
have been created at all, or rather does not
seem to have been invented. Shakespeare had
perhaps a model for Falstaff; he began with a
real man, but into him he was able to throw
the whole of his own mind, to feed his growth
with all his own faculties. Falstaff, belonging
to comedy, is a prose figure; but in him
Shakespeare raises prose to the height of
poetry, and then, in Hamlet, he enriches poetry

with the circumstance of prose. So we may
say of him that it is his peculiar achievement
to have fused poetry and prose, giving to each
the qualities of the other.

That may seem a mere formula for all that
passion and laughter and beauty, and it sounds
colder still to say of him that he more than
any other man has made poetry rational and
credible. Yet if we consider the beauty of his
poetry, the heights and depths of the soul to
which he attains, it is not cold. The greater
the weight of matter to be carried, the greater
is the power of flight needed to carry it; the
greater the mass of circumstance in a conception, the greater the imagination needed to
conceive it. Shakespeare's problem was the
problem of one who wrote for a living, of one
who loved life as it was too well to empty
it of content for artistic purposes; and yet it
was the problem of one who could not be
content without making a music out of life.
Words for him must perform all their ordinary
functions, yet they must dance; men and
women must have all the marks of circumstance
upon them, yet they must utter their immortal
souls; life must not be separated from its
routine and its indignities, yet it must overcome
them both with laughter and tears. This

problem he did not always solve, for he was a man, like all great artists, living desperately in a hand-to-mouth struggle, and not a god conceiving and executing without haste or rest. But it is his glory that he did live and work in such a way that he was able to solve this problem, the hardest that any writer ever set himself, more than once or twice. There are times when he rises from earth to heaven, trailing, not clouds of glory with him, but the whole diverse and troubled world of man, and because he ignores no element of that world, but transfigures it all in his music, he convinces us that his music is true. He was not a saint, but, more even than the saints, he charges our life with values, and when we have experienced *Hamlet* or *King Lear* we are utterly assured that life, whatever it brings us, is worth experiencing.

Shakespeare's Sonnets ☞ ☞ ☞

MANY people who do not care at all for poetry take an interest in Shakespeare's plays for irrelevant reasons. But you cannot take an irrelevant interest in the Sonnets unless you want to know who Mr. W. H. was, or who was the dark lady, which is absurd. The Sonnets are pure poetry, and also pure Elizabethan poetry. They belong to their time as much as Botticelli's Primavera. So, of course, do the plays; for the work of every great artist is rich with the character of his own time. It is only dull men, half conscious of their own dullness, who fear the vulgarity of circumstance and try to purge their writings of it. But the plays are so familiar to us, at least in quotations, that it is easy for us to mistake the Elizabethan in them for the universal. We think that all poetic plays ought to be like them. We are taught to see a kind of abstract perfection in them; and that teaching would make them seem dull if Shakespeare were not, luckily, the least dull of all great writers. As it is, when we forget that he was an Elizabethan we miss much of his character and beauty; for unless we understand what is temporal and local in a great artist, and see him, as it were, flowering in his native fields, we cannot enjoy him with perfect sincerity. His works cut off from their environment are like specimens in a botanical collection, and he seems to have written for libraries or painted for museums. How dull does the poetry of Shakespeare become when turned into maxims of universal application; and what a mass of dullness has been produced by versifiers trying to write plays like his in circumstances utterly different. The man who said that *Hamlet* was too full of quotations was wiser than he knew; it is often quoted by people who are not aware that it is either drama or poetry. But such people find little to quote in the Sonnets; and, though a few may read them to find out why Shakespeare wrote them, most of their readers are drawn to them by their poetry alone.

We may be sure that Shakespeare wrote his Sonnets for the pleasure of writing them. There was a good deal of task work in his early plays, as in the early journalism of Meredith; but in the Sonnets there was only the disinterested labour of a young artist, and afterwards of a master, turning from the business of his life to express himself directly. Among all the wild conjectures about the Sonnets one thing seems to be certain—namely, that many of the earlier ones were literary exercises and that many of the later were not. The theme at first seems artificial, and no doubt it was; the wise artist chooses an artificial theme when he is too young to get one from his own experience, for he knows that he must learn his art before he can use his experience of life in it. Besides, the young artist delights in his art for its own sake; it is still a pleasant game to him, and he is content that others should make the rules of it. Thus the young Shakespeare was glad to write like the other poets of the time; and, since sonnets, of one form or other, were the fashion, he wrote sonnets. No doubt he was less happy in his choice of a theme; we cannot be much interested in his arguments for marriage; they are only a pretext for writing poetry, and not a very good one. Besides, he sticks too conscientiously to his argument, so that we are provoked when we find that the wonderful opening—

Music to hear, why hear'st thou music sadly?
Sweets with sweets war not, joy delights in joy,

is only another incitement to matrimony. This is as near to being abstract poetry as any verse can be; the music has as little to do with the theme as the tunes of an Italian opera have to do with the situation.

But we are not therefore to suppose that Shakespeare wrote coldly, any more than Keats wrote coldly in Endymion. He was stirred by all the beauty of the world, and one beautiful thing brought another to his mind, as the scent of a flower reminds us of all the richness of summer. Nor did he write vaguely as many young poets write when moved by this general passion for beauty. The chief fault of his early verse—a promising fault in any young artist—is an excessive precision. Just as he labours description in Venus and Adonis, so he labours argument in the early Sonnets. He never trusts to luck or hopes that some meaning will come of a combination of fine sounds, but makes every word do as much work as if it were in a legal document. Indeed, all the legal terms which he uses are only a sign of his passion for precise expression; and if he had written nowadays he would very likely have pressed scientific words and images into his service. It is through his images that he is drawn more and more into reality and the

expression of his own experience.   Thus it may
be that, when in the twenty-first Sonnet he
glances at a rival poet, he is only following a
fashion; but continuing the same theme in
the twenty-third he starts by describing what
he must have often seen, and perhaps even felt
himself—

> As an unperfect actor on the stage,
> Who with his fear is put beside his part.

This has the sudden reality of Mercutio amid
all the romance of *Romeo and Juliet*.   Like
him, it is taken from life and foretells a poetry
in which romance and reality will be at one.

And soon the reality passes from images
into the main theme, enriching, not destroying,
the romance.   It is Shakespeare himself who
speaks of his own life in the sonnet which
begins, " When in disgrace with fortune and
men's eyes," not the Shakespeare of universal
fame, the imaginary tranquil master of all art
and knowledge, but one for whom, as for all
human beings, the future is uncertain and
failure as frequent as success.   We suppose
that anyone who could command the music
of Shakespeare or Schubert must have the
world at his feet; yet this music may have
been lavished on one indifferent individual, and

it only became the voice of universal passion when the authors of it were dumb. We might say of them as Shakespeare says of the unknown :—

> What is your substance, whereof are you made,
> That millions of strange shadows on you tend?

They who spoke so intensely for themselves seem now to speak for every one; and their music has gathered richness and meaning from the many times that it has been repeated as if it were uttered for the first time. But it only fits all passion because it fitted so exactly the passion that first begot it, and also because that passion itself was rich with the love of all beautiful things. No man whose love is narrow and confined to one single incident in his life can make poetry out of it; a man must have loved many things before he can express his love for one; otherwise he can only insist baldly that he loves, like the bandit in *Man and Superman* who cries :—

Mendoza thy lover,
Thy lover, Mendoza,
Mendoza adoringly lives for Louisa.
There's nothing but that in the world for Mendoza.
Louisa, Louisa, Mendoza adores thee.

The love poetry of Shakespeare is full of

delight because it is enriched and illustrated
with the love of many things.   When he asked
why his verse was "so far from variation or
quick change" he named the very qualities
for which it is most remarkable.   Yet all the
variations and quick changes are related to
each other because they express the same
passion for many different objects.   In this
the Sonnets are like *Love in the Valley*;
they show us a whole world heightened and
glorified by love. The interested passion of
one human being for another becomes part of
the disinterested passion for all beautiful things
and at the same time intensifies it so that the
poet can make as passionate a music about
summer as about love itself—

> Not that the summer is less pleasant now
> Than when her mournful hymns did hush
>   the night,
> But that wild music burthens every bough,
> And sweets grown common lose their dear
>   delight.

In the Sonnets, as in *Love in the Valley*, love
is no longer an incident in life, but a state
of being in which all things are harmonized;
and the world becomes one ideal landscape,
where every object has the same kind of

significance. It is a heaven of beauty, but not
a heaven of happiness; for, if it were, it would
be unreal, and we might believe those who say
that all the Sonnets are literary exercises.
That they are not, is proved by the very
sound of the poet's voice, which can be heard
in many of them as clearly as the voice of
Catullus in his finest verses.

> Never believe, though in my nature reign'd
> All frailties that besiege all kinds of blood,
> That it could so preposterously be stain'd,
> To leave for nothing all thy sum of good;
>   For nothing this wide universe I call,
>   Save thou, my rose; in it thou art my all.

This is as moving as the poem of Rochester's
in which he expresses the fear—

> Lest, once more wandering from that Heaven,
>   I fall on some base heart unblest,
> Faithless to thee, false, unforgiven,
>   And lose my everlasting rest.

True, Shakespeare's lines are full of the
Elizabethan rhetoric; but that was natural to
all poets of the time. It was a habit that had
become second nature; and it did not imply
the lack of real emotion any more than the
artificial phrases of an angry man nowadays

imply that his anger is feigned. The drama was the predominant form of poetry, and owing to its predominance all poetry tended to be rhetorical. The modern sonnet is apt to be meditative, as if the poet were thinking aloud in it; but the Elizabethan sonnet was written like a speech in a play, and it came naturally to Shakespeare to express himself like Berowne or Romeo, heightening his matter with all the arts that tell on the stage. No doubt he simplified the form of his sonnets to suit his dramatic manner. The Italian sonnet would have been too complicated and too slow in its movement for his eager eloquence, which would not endure to be checked at the end of the octave, and which, as it is, often seems to be violently reined in by the ·concluding couplet. All poetry is artificial in form, and the predominant artifice, whatever it may be, affects every poet's style, so that it seems more artificial than it is in an age subject to a different poetic convention. But Shakespeare in his finest sonnets is as much master of his rhetoric as in the finest scenes of his plays; and their peculiar merit is this, that in them all the Elizabethan eloquence becomes personal, like the whole apparatus of the orchestra in Beethoven's symphonies or the Florentine science in the drawings of Michelangelo.

> Ah, do not, when my heart hath 'scaped this sorrow,
> Come in the rearward of a conquered woe,
> Give not a windy night a rainy morrow,
> To linger out a purposed overthrow.
> If thou wilt leave me, do not leave me last,
> When other petty griefs have done their spite,
> But in the onset come ; so shall I taste
> At first the very worst of fortune's might.

The imagery of these lines is so subdued to the emotion that we scarcely notice it. A smaller artist would only weaken and dilute his passion with this comparison of his misfortunes to foul weather ; but here the result is to make the passion itself seem world-wide without losing any of its intensity. The current of the verse is so strong that it sweeps all the images along with it and they quicken the reader's imagination without troubling his understanding. His mind is never for a moment distracted from the main theme, yet that is enriched by a wild and various music which no simple and direct statement could contain. Shakespeare presses the wind and rain into his service, and turns their tempestuous sound into his own voice.

There are some great writers who are

naturally disposed to simplicity of expression.
Shakespeare was not one of these. Images
swarmed in his mind so that he had no need
to cast about for them ; indeed, he seems to
have thought in images. In modern times
thought is more abstract ; the scientific way
of thinking has affected pure literature, and
even the poets are shy of metaphor, lest it
should lead them into artifice and irrelevance.
But, though the profusion of Elizabethan
imagery may sometimes distract us from the
main theme, it is less artificial than we are apt
to suppose. Indeed, reasoning seems to have
grown out of the use of metaphor, just as prose
has grown out of poetry ; and much of the
Elizabethan imagery is a symptom of the
effort to reason in verse. Passion itself became argumentative then, as we may see from
the love poems of Donne ; no one doubts
that he expressed his own feelings, even in his
most flagrant conceits ; but because Shakespeare was a very great artist, his art, even at
its best, is supposed to prove that all through
the Sonnets he was only playing a brilliant
game. Sometimes, no doubt, he was. All
young poets, however full of passion, will write
for the mere pleasure of writing ; and passion
itself will incite them to elaborate every fancy

that comes into their minds. Nor is it strange that, in speaking for himself, Shakespeare should have kept some of his dramatic habits of speech. It is these very habits that give their eloquence to the Sonnets. The poet, used to set lovers talking on the stage, talks himself like Romeo ; but it is more reasonable to suppose that he knew how to make Romeo talk because he was himself a lover, than that he wrote the Sonnets because he had got the habit of expressing feigned passions on the stage.

The Prose Romances of William Morris

I

THE prose romances of William Morris, except those two which have a political purpose, are still little read. They have a few steady admirers, but most people, if they have heard of them at all, have formed a notion of them which keeps them from reading them. They think that Morris wrote them to illustrate some theory of his own about language or about beauty; that they are a protest against prosaic realism, or the ugliness of modern life, or what not. Others say that they are charming, no doubt, but shadowy and unreal, an inferior Earthly Paradise in prose, and there is quite enough of the real Earthly Paradise in verse. Well, the way to get rid of these notions is to read the romances themselves; and it is a very easy way. Begin with *The Wood beyond the World*, and, if you like romance at all, you will have finished it and started on another before you have asked yourself whether you enjoy it. There are some people, of course, who do not like romance at all, just as there are some who do not like music or pictures of the Madonna. They can be interested only in facts familiar to them, and they cannot believe any story that might not be told as news in a newspaper. But if these complain of the prose romances that they are vague or unsubstantial, they misstate the reason why they dislike them. It is true that Morris does not tell us when or where his stories happened, but he knows clearly and fully what happened in them, and he tells it with the precision of his knowledge. He never seems to be inventing, but always to be relating, and therefore it does not matter that he relates what may never have happened. Given the world of his romance, we know that it would have happened as he tells it.

A story, whatever kind of world it may be in, is, like the form of music, either a natural growth of the author's mind or a device; it is the result of his experience or of his desire to tell a story. Now it is commonly supposed that Morris's romances are the result of his desire to tell a story, or even of his desire to write in a certain style full of obsolete words and constructions. But Morris was a great man, and great men, whatever mistakes they may make, do not write for such reasons. It is true that in his prose romances he stole a holiday from his Socialism, but he did not change himself into a dilettante when he did that. The world of which he wrote, unlike the world in which he lived, was not one that he wished to reform; but neither was it, as some have absurdly called it, a decorative world. Literature cannot be decorative, for it is not a means of decoration; and to call it that, whether in praise or blame, is to use a false analogy. Probably those who call Morris's romances decorative mean that the characters in them are faintly drawn and move languidly against a background of pretty detail. If so, they have found in these romances what they expected to find, not what is there. For the romances are full of passion and trouble and delight and sin; and, although their world is not ours, it is a world in which Morris's own experience of life tells—indeed, it seems to be created entirely out of his experience. Perhaps the true reason why great artists turn to ideal art is to be found in the proper meaning of the word "ideal." It is not that they would empty their creation of all that is not beautiful in reality, but that they would make it all out of their own experience. Realism is a hindrance to them because it implies a mass of routine and detail which exists in reality but is not part of their experience of it. When Michelangelo painted "The Creation of Adam" he gave us, from his own experience of life, his notion of what life means to man. Clothes were not part of that meaning, nor were any circumstances of time and place; his Adam belongs to no age, and the ground on which he lies is of no season or country. Everything in the picture is created to express his idea and through it his experience. Michelangelo there was able to escape from irrelevant circumstance by means of his subject; and Morris uses romance for the same purpose. Unlike Michelangelo, he charges his romance with a great deal of circumstance, such as landscape and the handiwork of man; but all this he creates instead of copying it; and it is all there, not to make his romance like reality, but to express his own sense of values. Above all, it is not there for the sake of prettiness. Morris may have hated certain realities, but he did not fear them; and he did not turn to romance because he wished to persuade himself or anyone else that it was reality; he turned to it because he was able to express his own sense of reality most clearly in it.

Prose Romances of William Morris

II

I do not know how he made his stories; whether he invented them before he began to write, or whether they grew as he was writing. Probably they grew, for they read as if they were old stories, yet they are original and not like any old stories that we know. In all of them we feel the working of his mind, with his clear sense of the values of life and his wonder both at its beauty and at the mystery of its evil. There is magic in these stories, but it is not there to make them exciting, nor through any feeble attempt to believe in something incredible. We know that Morris did not believe in magic in this world; but in that world of his creation it seems to be equivalent to the mystery of evil in this. Evil, in this life, always seemed to him a malign enchantment; he could see far into the rational explanation of good things, but not of bad; he could understand imperfection, but not perversity. And his enchantresses in *The Wood beyond the World* and *The Water of the Wondrous Isles* are alive with this mystery of evil, with luxury and cruelty and the love of power, so that the power which they exercise seems to be evil itself, causeless, irrational, and ruinous, like evil in this world as he saw it. The enchantress in *The Wood beyond the World* destroys herself like evil, tempted to her death by enchantment, having stabbed one of her lovers who has taken the form of another.

But the Lady drew him toward her, and snatched the clothes from off his shoulders and breast and fell a-gibbering sounds mostly without meaning, but broken here and there with words. Then I heard her say: "I shall forget; I shall forget; and the new days shall come." Then there was silence of her for a little, and thereafter she cried out in a terrible voice: "O no, no, no! I cannot forget; I cannot forget"; and she raised a great wailing cry that filled all the night with horror (didst thou not hear it?), and caught up the knife from the bed and thrust it into her breast, and fell down a dead heap over the bed and on to the man whom she had slain.

But one can do no justice to these stories by quoting passages from them, for their life is in their movement and their effect is cumulative. What Morris tells sets the mind working so that it imagines things more wonderful than those which are told. The story is listened to breathlessly; and at the end the whole effect of it gathers upon the memory

as if it were single and instantaneous. But it
is worth quoting a passage to show how little
Morris's style resembles the common idea of
it. That idea is based upon a few sentences
which we wish he had written otherwise,
because they serve as an excuse for not reading
him. " Whilom, as tells the tale, was a walled
Cheaping-town hight Utterhay." So *The
Water of the Wondrous Isles* begins, and
people think that, because it begins so, it must
be a mere archaistic exercise. We wish that
he had not used obsolete words, since they distract the reader's attention from the sense,
but he did not use them because his sense was
poor. Those vices of style which are fatal are
also vices of matter, and Morris has not these.
His style is easier to understand than that of
most modern novelists, it is the style of a
writer who forgets himself in his story and
who forces neither beauty nor cleverness upon
us. It rises and falls with the matter, but
even where the matter is mere explanation it
is not dull or ugly.

III

These romances are remarkable, not for
their remote and tranquil beauty, but for their

vividness and precision. Morris, like Coleridge in *The Ancient Mariner*, is a realist of imagined things. He produces an illusion by showing us what we have never seen, not by reminding us of what we have seen. *The Well at the World's End* is a mediæval romance, but unlike other mediæval romances in that it seems to be told by a man who has lived in the Middle Ages. Scott, in *Ivanhoe* or *The Talisman*, insists upon strange and picturesque detail. He gives us stage scenery, and his characters, when they are not merely modern, act up to it. But Morris takes the Middle Ages as a matter of course; for him they are not scenery or a background, but the world in which his characters live and move, and the characters do not act their parts but are themselves. Nor does he tell us anything to remind us that we are in the Middle Ages; the details are there for the part they play in the story, they are details that one man of the time might have told to another, not as being strange, but as matters of common interest. Nor does he put his story in the Middle Ages because it is a beautiful time to him in which all goes well. He loves it, but not because he thinks of it as an earthly paradise. His sense of evil and oppression is just as strong when

he writes of the Burgh of the Four Friths
as when he writes of modern London. The
people of the Burgh are a kind of mediæval
Spartans, who oppress all their neighbours and
steal their women. They talk to a stranger
in an inn about these women, who are fairer
than their own, and one of them says that
they are " good websters, and, lacking them,
figured cloth of silk would be far-fetched and
dear-bought here." Thereupon a youth laughs
at him and says :—

Fair sirs, ye are speaking like hypocrites,
and as if your lawful wives were here to hearken
to you ; whereas ye know well how goodly
these thralls be, and that many of them can
be kind enough withal ; and ye would think
yourselves but ill bestead if ye might not
cheapen such jewels for your money. Which
of you will go to the Cross next Saturday and
there bring him a fairer wife than he can wed
out of our lineages ? and a wife withal of whose
humours he need take no more account than
of the dullness of his hound or the skittish
temper of his mare, so long as the thong
smarts and the twigs sting.

Here Morris shows us, the more vividly because
casually, the particular kind of oppression that
he most hated in all ages, the oppression
which treats human beings as if they were not

35

human; and he shows us, too, how this oppression, even in a strong military people, taints the whole of society and makes it ugly and loveless and luxurious. He was not writing a social tract, but expressing his own sense of values in a story; and it is that which makes his stories real to him and to his readers. Indeed, no romancer was ever less allured by the common elements of mediæval romance; he is not the fashionable novelist of the Middle Ages, interested in knights on horseback caracoling in search of adventure. Rather he loved the Middle Ages because they were expressive both of good and of evil, because both were plain to see in them, like the saints and devils of a Gothic church. What troubled him about our own time was its inexpressive complexity, its evil that seemed to be causeless, its good that produced evil results. Looking back on the Middle Ages, from a distance but with vast knowledge and still greater divination, he saw good and evil clearly opposed in them; and in his romances he could bring them to an issue and so for a while escape from his unsatisfied longing to bring them to an issue here and now. In *The Roots of the Mountains* there is war between the Goths, the people who were the hope of Europe, and the Huns, a mere force of barbarism and cruelty and destruction. To him that war is the prelude of the Middle Ages, and he tells of the victory of the Goths with the delight of one who knows what it means for the future. As we read, it seems to us, not a mere tale of fighting, but history told by one who took part in it yet had fore-knowledge of its meaning.

As for the people of the romances, they are not portraits, but rather figures in a large composition; yet they are never lay figures. Morris knew too well the kind of man and woman he liked not to draw them firmly. Now and again he surprises us by his subtlety though he never insists upon it, for his own mind was subtle. He had a turn for intro-spection which was checked by his incessant labours, but which taught him a great deal about other men's minds. This knowledge is usually rather implied than displayed, like so much of his knowledge; he is not an osten-tatious anatomist of the mind, but every stroke of character is firm and in its right place. His heroes and heroines are not insipidly good, but we know that we should like them if we could meet them, and we feel that there is much more to be known about them than he tells us. Indeed, we feel that about everything in the romances; he has created a world in them and not merely told a story, and there is that world of wonder and beauty and terror waiting to be enjoyed by thousands where it is now only enjoyed by tens.

Dickens ∽ ∽ ∽ ∽ ∽ ∽

(*Written for the Centenary of his birth*)

THE fourth part of Dickens's *Holiday Romance* tells of a country in which children and grown-ups change places. The children rule and the grown-ups have to obey them. The point of the story is that the grown-ups are described as if they were children, and being so described they appear more troublesome and less attractive than real children. There is a party of grown-ups at which

four tiresome, fat boys *would* stand in the doorway and talk about the newspapers, till Mrs. Alicumpaine [the child who gives the party] went to them and said, " My dears, I really cannot allow you to prevent people from coming in. I shall be truly sorry to do it ; but if you put yourselves in everybody's way I must positively send you home." One boy, with a beard and a large white waistcoat, who stood straddling on the hearthrug warming his coat-tails, *was* sent home. " Highly incorrect, my dear," said Mrs. Alicumpaine, handing him out of the room, " and I cannot permit it."

In this little tale Dickens only does openly and

consciously what he does, without knowing or without confessing it, in the best part of all his books. That boy with a beard and a large white waistcoat, who stood straddling on the hearth-rug, is seen as Dickens saw every one whom he did see, whether young or old, good or bad, male or female. His own life was not divided into periods of childhood, youth, and middle age; his experience was always of the same kind. People and things affected him to the last just as they had affected him when he first began to take notice; and since there were no divisions in his own life, he took no account of such divisions in the lives of others. He says, somewhere, that feelings which we think serious in a man seem to us comical in a boy; but he himself reversed the process. Children are nearly always serious to him. It is men who seem to him absurd, when they conceal their childishness behind beards and large white waistcoats. He loved those who, like himself, remained children all their lives; but the others seemed to him to be playing some kind of stupid game; and, if he could, he would have sent them all to bed.

What troubled him most in life was the fact that the pompous boys in beards and white waistcoats had all the power and used it to oppress the true children, young and old. He saw the Bumbles and Gradgrinds making life unpleasant for the poor, just as stupid grown-ups had made life unpleasant for him when he was a child. His own childish memory still smarts in his treatment of a mere tease like Pumblechook, against whom he pays off old scores as if they were scores of yesterday; and he hates Bumble as a boy might hate a bully at school. Thus, while he has great pity for those whom he loves and understands, he may seem merciless to those whom he does not; and there is a nursery morality in his punishments. There are two kinds of people in his books, the good and the bad, and at the end he sees that both get their deserts; but there is no real cruelty in his heaviest retributions. His villains are bundled off to gaol like guys to the bonfire, because it is the proper place for them. Fagin himself is half a guy, though real enough to be terrifying to a child; and we feel that Dickens has seen him as a frightened child might see him. So it is with Mr. Carker and even Madame Defarge; indeed, she talks as if she were talking to children with the aim of frightening them.

"You work hard, Madame," said a man near her.

" Yes," answered Madame Defarge. " I have a good deal to do."

" What do you make, Madame ? "

" Many things."

" For instance——"

" For instance," returned Madame Defarge composedly, " shrouds."

It reminds one of the Wolf in Red Riding-Hood, " All the better to eat you with, my dear."

Dickens's memory must have been stored with figures that had frightened him in his childhood, and at the same time excited his curiosity. His books are full of people vivid and sinister, who talk more or less incomprehensibly, who seem to have a secret way of life of their own and a nature, half elfish or devilish, half absurdly mechanical. That is how ugly people absorbed in their own concerns often appear to an observant child, who cannot from their speech discover what they are about, and who thinks, therefore, that it must be some wicked game played for its own sake. A child has no idea of business or the struggle for life ; it can be serious enough, but always over a game ; and it estimates people by the kind of game they seem to be playing and by the manner in which they play it. So Dickens saw all the different activities of men as games, good and bad. Wemmick, at the office, played a poor game; at home, with his castle and drawbridge and aged parent, he played a good one. Whenever Dickens chose he could forget all that he knew by experience about the struggle for life and fall into his natural childish observation of men's doings, describing them as if he did not know their object, with extreme vividness but with a constant sense of the absurdity of actions and words which seem mechanical because they are unintelligible. That was his satiric method, which he applied to officials, to people of fashion, to politicians, to all important persons. Every one who fell into routine, who seemed to act inexpressively and with no sense of the fun of life, was turned by him into a marionette. And in this world of marionettes, made vivid and strange by their isolation from the customary background of reason and purpose, animals and objects by way of compensation became more human, as they appear to the intense curiosity of a child. "The blackbeetles . . . groped about the hearth in a ponderous, elderly way, as if they were shortsighted and hard of hearing, and not on terms with one another." He thinks of them, too, as if they were playing a game, the game of pretending to be human beings, and he laughs at them for the serious manner in which they play it.

Naturally, with this method, he is better at invention than at construction. He took great pains with his plots, as with everything; but they often seem a mere distraction from his proper business. They provide motives for the behaviour of his vivid figures, motives which seem to us inadequate, as indeed they are, because they are manufactured, not observed like the figures themselves. For Dickens himself there was a perpetual mystery in human life, which he could enjoy without wishing to explain it. He was not a scientific novelist, and he only tried to be one to satisfy the supposed demands of his public. His natural way of telling a story was primitive: it was to relate the doings of men without troubling about their motives; and this he did so well that we believe in his characters without understanding them and without seeing any likeness in them to ourselves. Many of them have become mythical, and we are merely irritated when Dickens himself tries to rationalize his myths, to manufacture motives where he did not see them, as even Shakespeare manufactured motives for Iago which

are inadequate to explain him. Dickens's
business is creation, not analysis, and he
creates so profusely that his creatures often
become an unmanageable mob who will not be
governed by his plot. What has Mrs. Gamp
to do with the plot of *Martin Chuzzlewit* or
with the world of duty and business with
which he makes a feeble effort to connect her?
If we could for a moment consider the motives
of her conduct, she would dwindle into a
wicked old woman; but Dickens had seen her
and drawn her without a thought of her
motives. She has nothing to do with right
and wrong, and the fact that she is a nurse
is a mere pretext for her introduction. All
we ask of her is that she shall continue to talk;
and we follow her through the book as we
follow a great comic actor when he gags upon
the stage. Both may interfere with the plot,
but, if they do, so much the worse for it.
When Falstaff enters, the history of England
becomes a mere background to him; and when
Mrs. Gamp is talking, Martin Chuzzlewit is
a super.

There is only one other English novelist who
for limitations and for intensity can be compared with Dickens—namely, Charlotte Brontë;
and there is a similar cause for the limitations

and the intensity of both. For as Dickens is the child among novelists, Charlotte Brontë is the girl. They see very differently, but the eyes of both are not dulled by experience and their feelings not blunted by theory. They do not find in life what they expect to find in it, and therefore their books are full of surprises for us. But experience is a word that may be used in different senses. People have wondered that Charlotte Brontë should have written so well with so little of it; they forget that it was a sharp experience for her to meet a new person or to enter a room for the first time. We cannot tell whether she would have kept this eagerness of perception if she had lived; but Dickens kept it all his life, and he is her only rival in describing everything as if he had never seen anything like it before. The difference between them is a difference both of sex and of age. She is older than he is, for there is nothing childlike about her. Both are magnificently unworldly; but Dickens went through the world with a child's detachment, watching it and wondering at it, working too hard, enjoying himself too much, but never turning his game into a business. Charlotte Brontë was not detached from life, but caught into it by newborn passions and instincts. She had reached the age of love, and the world was as full of adventures for her as it was full of men. For Dickens, being still a child, it was as full of adventures as of things. Adult love to him is only a tiresome business that has to be written about because his readers, being grown up, want it. For Charlotte Brontë it is the one thing that gives meaning and a fearful glory to life. But with this difference between them they are alike in this and unlike other great novelists, that they always seem to write about the present, not the past. Nothing that they tell of is mellowed or dimmed by the lapse of time; as we read them we have the same illusion of something that has just happened, the same conviction of reality, unsupported by reason and defiant of it, which comes to us when we remember in the morning a dream of last night. Other writers have to satisfy our sense of probability; their fiction must be less strange than truth because they must persuade us that it is true; but Dickens and Charlotte Brontë can persuade us of anything by their mere power of representation. As we read them we see with their eyes and pass through their experiences. It may be all subjective, as the philosophers say; but so is a dream, and that is often more vivid than objective realities.

Charlotte Brontë has this one advantage over Dickens, that love for her is a predominating interest to which all other interests are subordinate. So she can make a story out of love, coherent and of natural growth, with all her own rebellions against it and misunderstandings of it, with the conflict between it and the sense of duty, religion, conventions, the struggle for life. Her very situation is so interesting that it makes a novel by itself. For her, the passionate girl of genius trained in a country parsonage, life is all a voyage of discovery and every incident an adventure. The contact between her mind and the world is so sharp that sparks are struck from it every moment. As we read her books we think only of her; we do not see her characters as they are, but feel them as she felt them. Dickens is not thus the centre of his books, nor does love make a plot for him. Indeed, love, as he naturally represents it, is only a childish wistfulness soon forgotten in the struggle of life. It is almost the only thing that he seems to describe as a faint memory, calling it by an effort out of the past as other writers call up their childhood. But he has this advantage over Charlotte Brontë, that his interests are far more diverse than hers. Like a child, he can forget himself in the spectacle of life. She judges everything—and rather harshly—except passion. His natural inclination is to judge nothing and to enjoy everything, even the bores and the humbugs. The world of humour is closed to her and the world of passion to him. There are distressing passages in the works of both: in hers when she thinks it necessary for her characters to be funny; in his when his characters try to make love or talk about love like grown-up people. And it is a curious fact that her fun and his sentiment read very much alike; there is the same preposterous artificiality in both, the same instant loss of all those great qualities of style which elsewhere they exhibit so constantly.

There used to be a notion, founded on his sentimental failures, that Dickens was an illiterate vulgarian of genius, a bad and unscrupulous writer who interests the refined only because he tells them of vulgar people like himself whom they have never met. But no one who has ever tried to write can read a chapter of him without seeing that he was master of a sound and even classical prose style. It is true that he had not what we call a classical education; but he was as well trained for writing English novels as Æschylus for writing Greek plays. His teachers were Fielding, Smollett, and Defoe; and he had learned from them thoroughly. If he felt and saw like a child, he wrote like a man, with a masculine weight and clearness and balance. There is no hysteria in his pamphlets, but moderation and common sense, and anger only when it is just. He was not naturally rhetorical or sentimental, but supplied both rhetoric and sentiment out of conscientious good-nature. They were sweetmeats that he did not like himself, but gave to his grown-up readers because they clamoured for them. When we call him a child we do not impute to him any weakness of intellect or lack of judgment; he was limited only in his range of emotions and in his appreciation of adult motives; and even that limitation was the result, perhaps, of his extreme keenness of perception. We cannot believe that he was incapable of any kind of emotion or understanding whatever; but his mind was so busy with the material provided for it by his eyes and ears that it had no leisure to occupy itself with its own workings or to entertain a lasting passion.

Dickens

Yet the dazzling spectacle of life did inspire him with one lasting passion—the passion of pity; and it was that which gave music to his laughter and weight to his thought. All his ideas were sound; he loved the essential virtues and hated the essential vices. If life could be as he wished it to be, it would be neither dull nor cruel; there would be room in it both for the weak and for the strong, for the city clerk and the man of genius. We can best understand a great writer by noticing what he does best; and Dickens's masterpiece is not Mrs. Gamp, nor even Peggotty or Joe Gargery, but the convict Abel Magwitch. It was not fun but pity that lifted his genius to its greatest height, and a pity as reasonable as justice. There is no description of his so sharp and so full of meaning as the description of Magwitch as Pip first saw him on his return :—

In all his ways of sitting and standing, and eating and drinking—of brooding about, in a high-shouldered, reluctant style—of taking out his great horn-handled jack-knife and wiping it on his legs and cutting his food—of lifting light glasses and cups to his lips, as if they were clumsy pannikins—of chopping a wedge off his bread, and soaking up with it the last fragments of gravy round and round his plate,

as if to make the most of an allowance, and
then drying his fingers on it, and then
swallowing it—in these ways and a thousand
other small nameless instances arising every
minute in the day, there was Prisoner, Felon,
Bondsman, plain as plain could be.

In that description, and in the account of
the process by which Pip's first disgust was
changed to affection, Dickens is no longer the
marvellous child among novelists but a master
among those masters who have taught pity
to the world out of their own hearts. And
his pity here is too proud and too sure of itself
to argue. There may have been readers when
Great Expectations was published who thought
that the account of the death sentence was an
appeal to sentiment, that it was only a proper
protection of society that men and women
should be hanged by scores for all sorts of
offences, and in particular for returning to
their native country when they had been transported for life. But read the passage now
and you will think Dickens's pity wiser than
their common sense :—

Penned in the dock . . . were the two-and-
thirty men and women ; some defiant, some
stricken with terror, some sobbing and weeping,
some covering their faces, some staring gloomily

Dickens

about. There had been shrieks from among the women convicts, but they had been stilled, and a hush had succeeded. The sheriffs with their great chains and nosegays, other civic gewgaws and monsters, criers, ushers, a great gallery full of people — a large theatrical audience—looked on, as the two-and-thirty and the Judge were solemnly confronted.

Then follows the Judge's address to Magwitch, with its reasons why he deserved to die, all based upon a gross ignorance of his character and motives. In the person of that Judge, Dickens reveals the world to itself with an irony more quiet and more deadly than laughter or tears. There his genius, wise in its childishness, spoke with the voice of posterity; and it seems to speak now as if he were living among us and could rebuke us too for our pompous cruelties and could, like the child that he was, enjoy the praise and honour we give to his memory.

Algernon Charles Swinburne ⌒ ⌒

(Written on the occasion of his death)

WHEN a great poet dies it is natural and right that we should think only of the splendour and not of the imperfection of his works. While he is with us, and when we have grown accustomed to his presence among us, we may note the defects of his genius; and these are sure to be judged by the unconscious but implacable justice of posterity. At the moment of his death we must feel and express only our gratitude for all that he has done to glorify our lives. Then, for a while, he has no competitors among the living or the dead. The thoughts of all lovers of poetry are fixed upon him, as the thoughts of a family are fixed upon a member of it who has just passed away.

There is no doubt that Algernon Charles Swinburne was one of our great poets, a master of his art who said immortal things and helped to make the history of the human mind. But there is one circumstance that makes his death peculiarly moving to us. He

Algernon Charles Swinburne

was the last of the giant race before the flood, the latest born and the latest to survive of the great romantic poets who have dominated our literature ever since the first songs of Blake rose almost unheard so long ago. The death of Swinburne marks the close of an heroic age in our poetry, as the death of Tintoret marked the close of an heroic age in Italian art. True, there is one of Swinburne's great companions who still survives; but as a poet Mr. George Meredith is troubled with our later emotional scepticism. He is in date a romantic, as Donne was an Elizabethan; but, like Donne, he has always been in revolt against the poetry of his own time and has seemed to be making experiments towards the poetry of the future. He is, as it were, wandering between two worlds, labouring to make an instrument for the expression of ideas still too new to be expressed in terms of beauty. But Swinburne belonged altogether to a world of poetry that has died with him. In literature he was the heir of all the ages, and the last inheritor of a great tradition. There are some great men who prepare for the future and others who consummate the past. He was one of these; he seems to have been born with the ideas that informed all his poetry, or at least to have acquired them without effort or question. There was never any emotional scepticism in him; he had never to persuade himself of the value of what he loved or the worthlessness of what he hated. No poetry has less argument than his or less prosaic content. About the glories of life he was an extreme dogmatist, and his one aim in poetry was to express them. Thus from us, with our emotional insecurity, our constant questioning of the values of all things, he is as far removed as Fra Angelico; and as a poet he seems to have the unfair advantage of the artists of the age of faith. It makes no difference that his faith sometimes expressed itself in furious denunciation; he was as eager to proclaim his disbeliefs as his beliefs and he made poetry out of both. Whatever his superficial extravagances or perversities may have been, he knew for certain what he valued in life; his mind was fixed and his faith unshaken.

There still persists a notion that he was a morbid poet. In his youth he played with morbidities, as boys play at being pirates; but they never tainted his mind or perverted his sense of the value of things. They were mere experiments, like some of his versification;

Algernon Charles Swinburne

and, like all men of enormous and restless
energy, he was fond of experiments in his art.
He spoke afterwards of certain poems in the
first series of *Poems and Ballads* as the sins
of his youth. In the Prelude to *Songs
before Sunrise* he said that he had done with
them and was now to treat of loftier themes.
We have, he wrote,

> A little time that we may fill
> Or with such good works or such ill
>   As loose the bonds or make them strong
>   Wherein all manhood suffers wrong.
> By rose-hung river and light-foot rill
>   There are who rest not; who think long
> Till they discern as from a hill
>   At the sun's hour of morning song,
> Known of souls only, and those souls free,
> The sacred spaces of the sea.

He himself was never in doubt which works
were good and which ill; and his eyes were
always set steadfastly upon the sacred spaces of
the sea. He was not content to rest, or to
prolong the emotions and the music of his
youth past their proper season. There is
another poem of his in which he says
farewell to his youth, and no poet has ever
said it more bravely. We are all of us, when
the change to middle age comes, afflicted with
a sense that the glory of life has passed away;

and poets are sometimes overpowered by that sense, and cry—"Out of the day and night a joy hath taken flight." Swinburne got a new inspiration from the courage with which he faced the change. In the Vision of Spring in Winter he says :—

The morning song beneath the stars that fled
  With twilight through the moonless mountain
    air,
  While youth with burning lips and wreathless
    hair
Sang toward the sun that was to crown his head,
Rising; the hopes that triumphed and fell dead,
  The sweet swift eyes and songs of hours that
    were;
These mayst thou not give back for ever; these,
  As at the sea's heart all her wrecks lie waste,
      Lie deeper than the sea;
But flowers thou mayst, and winds, and hours of
    ease,
  And all its April to the world thou mayst
    Give back, and half my April back to me.

There are not many of us who know the hopes that triumph and fall dead, whose dreams of world-wide fame come true before they are thirty; and it is difficult for us to understand that a poet cannot live for ever upon dreams come true. Swinburne discovered that by experience; he faced the fact and

Algernon Charles Swinburne

determined to take all the seasons of life as they came. Therefore he did not outlive his gift or his faith, but learned to write better of death than he had ever written of love :—

> The seal of sleep set on thine eyes to-day
> Surely can seal not up the keen swift light
> That lit them once for ever. Night can slay
> None save the children of the womb of night.

These lines are from the elegy on John William Inchbold, which was published in the third series of *Poems and Ballads*. That poem and others in the book are enough to refute the common belief that Swinburne's genius spent itself in his youth, that after thirty he never said anything that he had not said better before. The belief exists, perhaps, because there are no signs of struggle or doubt or transition in his work. He always had the voice of youth and wrote like a lover; but as he grew older he wrote less and less of the passions of youth and more and more of the matters that concern, or should concern, manhood. He was never a great tragic poet, hard as he tried to be one, for his genius was lyrical; but there have been few poets who could treat a tragic theme lyrically as well as he, none who has revived the ballad with such a perfect mixture of nature and art. Here is a verse from *A Jacobite's Exile* :—

> We'll see nae mair the sea-banks fair,
>   And the sweet grey gleaming sky,
> And the lordly strand of Northumberland,
>   And the goodly towers thereby ;
> And none shall know but the winds that blow
>   The graves wherein we lie.

And here is one, even more poignant, from *A Jacobite's Farewell* :—

> O lands are lost and life's losing,
>   And what were they to gie?
> Fu' mony a man gives all he can,
>   But nae man else gives ye.

Critics have talked of Swinburne's wonderful power of imitation, as if he were a mere virtuoso producing a series of literary exercises. The best answer to that kind of criticism is to read *Before the Beginning of Years* or *A Jacobite's Exile*, and then to ask whether any imitative poetry has ever rung like that. There is the same golden music in both ; and that music expresses something great in the poet's soul, a divine energy of emotion not hampered by doubt or chilled by fear. It is often said that his poetry contains nothing but music ; it would be as foolish to say of music itself that it contains nothing but music ; for

all real music, whether of words or of notes,
expresses a real emotion. We are apt not to
give a man credit for what he can do with
magnificent ease; and it is hard to realize all
the learning and labour and high thinking and
noble feeling that have gone to the making of
that rushing music. Often it is so swift that
we scarcely notice the thought latent in it.
The impetus of the sound will not suffer our
minds to dwell on the sense. But still the
sense is there in all his finer poems, and he
himself has warned us of the fact in a beautiful image :—

For life's helm rocks to the windward and lee,
And time is as wind, and as waves are we ;
　And song is as foam that the sea-winds fret,
Though the thought at its heart should be deep as
　　the sea.

Swinburne was never an "intellectual." He
was too sure of things for that, and had too
simple a delight in life and his art. But only
those who know nothing of poetic processes
would call him a brainless poet. He did not
argue or analyse, because he held that he had
something better to do ; but we can see from his
criticism that his theory of poetry was clear
and consistent. Poetry for him was a means of
expressing emotion in terms of beauty ; it

might do other things, but they were not essential. The emotion and the material beauty were essential, the one being the expression of the other. No doubt he carried this theory to an extreme in his practice; he was too determined to express emotion in every line and to make every line beautiful ever to write a good play or a good narrative poem. All the people in his plays make poetry about the situation; they do not live and move and have their being in it, and *Tristram of Lyonesse* is a series of magnificent distractions from the story. But in the plays he speaks sometimes like a great tragic poet, although he can never manage the action about which he speaks. Here is the end of *Locrine*, in which Gwendolen, having defeated and killed her husband and his paramour in battle, says that she will not refuse them burial :—

Not I would sunder tomb from tomb
Of these twain foes of mine, in death made one—
I, that when darkness hides me from the sun
Shall sleep alone, with none to rest by me.
But thou—this one time more I look on thee—
Fair face, brave hand, weak heart that wast not mine—
Sleep sound—and God be good to thee, Locrine.
I was not. She was fair as heaven in spring
Whom thou didst love indeed. Sleep, queen and king,
Forgiven ; and if—God knows—being dead, ye live,
And keep remembrance yet of me—forgive.

Algernon Charles Swinburne

To show what variety there is to be found in this poet, often called monotonous, we will quote a passage in the same metre from the description of the loves of Tristram and Iseult :—

                              Like fire
The lit dews lightened on the leaves, as higher
Night's heart beat on toward midnight. Far and
    fain
Somewhiles the soft rush of rejoicing rain
Solaced the darkness, and from steep to steep
Of heaven they saw the sweet sheet lightning leap
And laugh its heart out in a thousand smiles,
When the clear sea for miles on glimmering miles
Burned as though dawn were strewn abroad astray,
Or, showering out of heaven, all heaven's array
Had paven instead the waters.

In passages like this, and, indeed, in the whole poem, romantic poetry exhausts its possibilities. The romantic process of combining human passions and natural forces in one complicated harmony could not be carried any further, nor could the appropriate romantic effects of versification. No further development is possible in the art of poetry as Swinburne practised it. He has had a few imitators, but only one notable follower. Professor Gilbert Murray, translating the most romantic of Greek poets, has divined, perhaps almost unconsciously, that he could not do justice to the art of his original, except with an art no less highly wrought. If there had been any dullness or crudity in the language and verse of his translation, it must have failed altogether. There was only one contemporary style equal to the task, and that was the style of Swinburne. The success of the translator proves, not only his own genius, but the greatness of both his originals. The mind of Euripides is equal to the language of Swinburne, and the language of Swinburne to the mind of Euripides. There is also a pleasant irony in the feat, since Swinburne's hatred of Euripides was one of his few critical perversities.

Hitherto, we fear, we may seem to have made too many apologies for the great poet. That is the worst of criticism, it must be always either detracting or apologizing; to express the glory of a master is beyond the powers of any critic. The final question to be put about a poet is this—Has he increased our sense of the value of the noble things of life? To do that is the function of all art, not by argument but by expression. Therefore, in considering what we owe to the genius of Swinburne, we should not ask what ideas we have got from him, but what emotions, and of what nature and strength; for emotion is our final test of the values of things. To this question there can be only one answer. Those who are familiar with his greatest works know that they communicate noble emotions with irresistible power; his music puts us in love with life; and we can only love the best of life. Even in that earlier poetry of his that seems all melodious despair, it is really the thwarted and troubled glory of life that he sings. The music of *Before the Beginning of Years* is exultant, whatever the sense may be. In his poetry, life, freed from all routine and irrelevance, is represented in music as a conflict of vast significance between good and evil forces, and the evil forces, like Milton's Satan, have splendour and greatness. Even when Swinburne hates he never sneers; and his invective, however extreme, is like the shadow cast by a bright light. What is it that we remember of his two sonnets to the White Tsar? Not what he denounces, but what he glorifies; not the abuse, but the passage in which he tells the Tsar to take heed lest his crownless head lie low :—

By his of Spain who dared an English Queen
With half a world to hearten him for fight,
Till the wind gave his warriors and their might
To shipwreck and the corpse-encumbered sea.

No doubt he could hate, and exulted sometimes in expressing his hatred. But his
genius lay not in hatred, but in love; and his
noblest poems are those which express love of
what is best worth loving. All greatness and
beauty, whether of nature or of man, fired him;
he was like the legendary statue that burst
into music when touched by the rays of the
sun. In the sestet of his finest sonnet he
praised two leaders who seemed to him to
refuse the highest hopes of mankind, and
with this we will end instead of praising him
further :—

Honour not hate we give you, love not fear,
    Last prophets of past kind, who fill the dome
Of great dead Gods with wrath and wail, nor hear
    Time's word and man's : "Go honoured hence,
        go home,
Night's childless children ; here your hour is done ;
Pass with the stars, and leave us with the sun."

The Wonderful Visitor ◡ ◡ ◡

MR. GOSSE was born, and bred, to write the life of Swinburne; and it is a piece of luck for the immediate reputation of the poet. An official biography would have made him seem uninteresting to all the young; they would have glanced at it, said "Just what I thought," and read his poems no more. But you cannot glance at this book without reading it through; and having read it, you will wish to read the poems again. To treat Swinburne in an official manner would be like breaking a Bird of Paradise on the wheel; and never for a moment has Mr. Gosse attempted to do so. There is a Swinburne legend which would have been killed by an official biography, but Mr. Gosse authenticates it for us; he convinces us that our most delightful dreams about the poet were true, and that the truth is even better than the dreams. Could a book full of so much good fun have been written about any other great poet? Hogg came near it in his fragment of a life of Shelley; but the family suppressed him, and throughout his book the fun is marred by a sense of insecurity. Shelley is always a tragic figure, tragic for others as well as himself; but Swinburne's life is like summer lightning.

I do not mean that Mr. Gosse makes him seem futile or ridiculous. Love and admiration are implied in everything he says; but he is not going to make the poet insipid; his aim is to give us his exact and exquisite quality, which he does in a number of stories, a number of delicate phrases, all carried on in the quiet stream of his narrative. He does not criticize the poems much, though what he says of them is both just and amusing; but, after reading his book, we shall understand them better and enjoy them more. For he shows us the connexion between the solemn, august part of the poet and his childishness; he makes the two one; and until we see them as one we cannot do him justice.

Swinburne was a wonderful visitor to this earth, like Mr. Wells's angel; he was like an angel of Florentine fifteenth-century art, impish and beautiful, and the more beautiful because impish. Every story about him is in character, like the stories about Mozart; he ought himself to have been in *The Magic Flute*, and to have played his tricks and sung his divine songs in that paradise of music. He was often absurd, and yet always in character, with an absurdity which his friends loved because it was his, for it was beautiful, like a child's errors of speech. It makes one laugh, but never with a sense of superiority over him ; and it is also pathetic, for he was always losing his way like a child in the world, and until Watts-Dunton became his nurse there was no one to look after him. Mr. Gosse expresses the pathos of it in the most delicate way. He tells us, for instance, of an evening in 1877, when Swinburne was forty, but still a child. He went to Swinburne's rooms to hear him read the essay on Charlotte Brontë :—

Algernon was standing alone in the middle of the floor, with one hand in the breast of his coat and the other jerking at his side. He had an arrangement of chairs, with plates and glasses set on the table, as if for a party. He looked like a conjuror who was waiting for his audience. He referred vaguely to " the others," and said that, while they delayed in coming, he would read me a new poem he had just finished. . . . The poem was very magnificent, but rather difficult to follow, and very long. It took some time to read ; and still no one came. As the evening was slipping away I asked him presently whether the reading of C. Brontë should not begin. Whereupon he answered, "I'm expecting Watts and Ned Burne-Jones and Philip Marston, and—some other men. I hope they'll come soon." We waited a little while in silence, in the twilight, and then Swinburne said, "I hope I didn't forget to ask them." He then trotted or glided into his bedroom, and what he referred to there I don't know, but almost instantly he came out and said cheerfully, "Ah! I find I didn't ask any of those men, so we'll begin at once." After he had read long and with amazing violence "he seemed quite exhausted, and sank into a kind of dream into the corner of his broad sofa, his tiny feet pressed tight together, and I stole away."

Life was as dangerous to him as to a child, and yet he passed through it, as he passed through London traffic, though he seemed in danger of being run over every moment. But on one point the common legend about him does him an injustice, like the common opinion of his poetry; it does injustice to his intellect. He had, as Mr. Gosse says, great *savoir-faire* and a very shrewd judgment of character. If he had wished to be a man of the world he might have been one. He could understand whatever he wished to understand, like Shelley,

and he had more sympathy than Shelley.
No one has ever done justice to the subtlety
of his novel *Love's Cross Currents*; and
even Mr. Gosse only mentions it by name.
But in it he shows a power, like that of Henry
James, to give us the very scent of character, a
power which he left undeveloped in his poetry.
He was also, unlike the minor poets who tried
to imitate him, a hard worker and a great
scholar. "He is," Ruskin said in 1866,
"simply one of the mightiest scholars of his
age in Europe." Further, as Mr. Gosse points
out, there is in *Songs before Sunrise* a
philosophic power beyond that of any other
poet of the time. But the music of these
poems is so loud that it drowns the thought
in them; and every one said, and still says,
that he was merely a singer with a wonderful
organ. That belief was encouraged by his
impishness; we expect a great poet to be
solemn, and Swinburne could be solemn only
with a child's insecurity; at any moment he
would turn to the game of abusing those whom
he delighted to abuse, and the more fiercely
he did it the more it was a game to him.

All rage and bitterness were a game to him,
which he learnt from Victor Hugo. "From
his satirical poems," says Mr. Gosse, "he

adopted a certain attitude of being astride the barricades of existence, shouting at the top of his voice with a flambeau in his fist. It was inconsistent with the dignity, gentleness, and docility which were also natural to him." Yes, it is a distressing fact about children that they will incessantly shout. It spoils the music of their voices, and often it spoiled the music of Swinburne's, and also drowned his thought. Mr. Gosse tells us plainly that he was·never fit to live at liberty in London; but he had this great good fortune, and also merit, that, whatever his "irregularities" when he was there, he could always return home to his family like a child that has hurt itself; and at home he was a happy and peaceful child. In 1871 Henry Kingsley wrote, in a letter, of his behaviour with his father and mother. "I believe Algy is very eccentric in London, but I never see him there. Here he is a perfectly courteous little gentleman." So it was natural to write of the divine poet and the man of thirty-four; his father said of him: "God has endowed my son with genius, but He has not vouchsafed to grant him self-control." One can see that to his parents he was always a child, and also that he was content to be a child to them and to love them like a child;

yet, when his father died, he wrote a poem about him that will make his name immortal.

Mr. Shaw has said somewhere that Swinburne wrote about literature poetry almost as good as other poets have written about life. That seems a just condemnation of the poet —until you read his best poetry. Then the problem is—What was the nature of the power which produced this poetry? Mr. Gosse's book helps us to solve it. We see that Swinburne, whatever else he may have been, was not one who exploited himself for literary purposes. To talk of his marvellous technical gifts as if they were separate from his mind and character is to fall into a dangerous error about him and about the nature of art. Only a great poet has marvellous technical gifts in poetry; and a man can be a great poet only with the whole of himself. Swinburne did not, as critics have supposed, experience life at two removes; but life was very much simplified to him, as it is to most children. Like them, he believed always that he could have his heaven here and now on this earth; and what was not heaven to him was hell. His heaven here and now was peopled with saints and angels, and his hell with devils; not devils that he really hated or feared, but a gargoyle kind of devil, for which he delighted to find invective. He enjoyed them almost as much as his angels, enjoyed telling them what he thought of them, as a mediæval sculptor enjoyed carving gargoyles. He saw life as an incessant war between them and his angels, in which the angels always triumphed like Michael over the dragon; and he sang the songs of triumph.

Some of those songs, like other religious exercises, are long and tiresome; they are like the Athanasian Creed set to Handelian music. But he could praise more magnificently than any poet that has ever lived, like a choir of Correggio's young-eyed cherubim. To think of his gift for music as if it were physical like a great voice is to be lost in a false analogy; his music was the answer of his spirit to the universe, of a reality in him to a reality outside him. There was ritual in it, as if he were a young priest, an Ion, of the universe; he waved his censer, he made his obeisances, he raised his chant; and there are times when we wish our poets to be men talking, not priests chanting. For Swinburne all life was a wonderful memory, not a sudden surprising discovery. His heroes, even while he stood face to face with them,

were legendary to him; Mazzini was like
Harmodius, Victor Hugo like Æschylus; the
past ordered the present for his mind; he lived
not in time but in a—

> Steadfast rest of all things firmly stayed
> Upon the pillars of eternity;

and his very impishness and naughtiness were
but a refusal to have any dealings with the
transitory and particular. The universal
alone existed for him; and his is a poetry of
the universal, both in its themes and in its
method. It is all religious poetry as much as
the poetry of Crashaw; the only difference
is in the subject-matter. He writes about
Mazzini as Crashaw writes about St. Theresa;
and about the Republic as Crashaw writes
about the Name above every name, the Name
of Jesus. You may call either poet empty,
vague, artificial, if you will and are deaf to
their music; but this music expresses a universal that cannot be expressed otherwise in
words, and one of which they were actually
aware in their own experience. They themselves remained young-eyed cherubim through
all the routine of life; and if we will not listen
to their music, that is our loss.

Swinburne did not grow old like other men.

He merely became aware of the fact that he needed a nurse, and retired into the safe nursery that Watts-Dunton made for him at Putney. Watts-Dunton had the weaknesses common to the best of nurses: he was over-officious, over-watchful, over-eager to keep his charge from playing with bad boys who might lead him into mischief, and he tried to teach him his own very domestic wisdom. This, too, often, Swinburne accepted like a good child, and recanted his old admirations with the old childish vehemence. Mr. Gosse, very naturally, is a little impatient of this nursery tyranny; but it must have prolonged the poet's life, and he was happy and healthy under it. "He went on gliding over the commons of Wimbledon with the old noiseless regularity, but it could hardly be said that he held a place any longer in the ordinary world around him." More than ever he lived on memories; and his later poetry seems all to be made out of the memories of his youth. But we think that Mr. Gosse, like every one else, is unjust to it. It is not all the poetry of mere momentum and habit. If the lines on John William Inchbold, in the third series of *Poems and Ballads*, had appeared in the first, they would be famous; but the world had made up its mind that

The Wonderful Visitor

Swinburne was only echoing himself, and it listened to him no longer. Perhaps some foolish people will think that Mr. Gosse has not been reverent enough to him; but there is in his book that reverence which does not fear to tell the affectionate truth.

Donne's Sermons ✍ ✍ ✍ ✍

THERE is a legend that Donne was the greatest of English preachers, but even those who read old books, even those who read his poetry, do not read his sermons. Mr. Pearsall Smith has made a selection from them and he begins by telling us why they are unread. There are very many of them, they are very long; and Donne had "the unhappy faculty of developing to the utmost the faults of any form of literary expression he adopted." The worst fault of the sermon, as literature, is that it is preaching. We make it a reproach against writers when they preach, not merely because preaching is out of place except in sermons, but because in itself it is disagreeable. We do not like a man who preaches, in the pulpit or out of it; for in the process he ceases to be human—men are not born to preach to each other—he loses the good faith of the artist, he tells us not what he has to say, but what

78

he thinks we ought to hear. The convention
of sermons changes, but it is never a good one ;
it is always a giant's robe, awkwardly worn by
men as dwarfish as the rest of us. When he
enters the pulpit the priest must pretend to
be a prophet ; however humble he be by
nature, that pretence makes him speak with
alien jaws, louder than his wont, with a
solemnity not his and a conviction he has not
earned. Some few of us read sermons of to-
day because we are used to their convention
and hope they will do us good; but we do not
read sermons of yesterday, or of the seven-
teenth century. As Mr. Pearsall Smith puts
it, they seem to belong to some remote
geological era of human thought.

But he has read Donne's sermons more than
once, and he has found in them, like an
excavator among palæolithic remains, fragments of art, of eloquence, of passion. The
great poet was not lost in the preacher, but
transmuted; Donne himself says, thinking no
doubt of his own case, that a voluptuous man,
turned to God, will " find plenty and delicious-
ness enough in him, to feed his soul, as with
marrow, and with fatness, as David expresses
it ; and so an angry and passionate man will
find zeal enough in the house of God to eat

him up." The example he gives is obsolete to us, but it must have been apt enough to him.

Solomon, whose disposition was amorous, and excessive in the love of women, when he turn'd to God, departed not utterly from his old phrase and language, but having put a new, and a spiritual tincture, and form and habit in all his thought, and words, he conveys all his loving approaches and applications to God, and all God's gracious answers to his amorous soul, into songs, and Epithalamians, and meditations upon contracts, and marriages between God and his Church, and between God and his soul.

We may smile at the notion that it was a converted Solomon who sang the Song of Solomon, but the converted Donne did continue to sing even in the pulpit; he could not be subdued to what he worked in; and Mr. Pearsall Smith has rescued these beauties and made an anthology of them, saving us all the pains that he has taken and we could never have endured.

Donne is here one of the greatest of our prose writers, in some things unequalled. The sermons are not written as they were preached; he took no fully written manuscript into the pulpit, Mr. Pearsall Smith tells us, but wrote from memory afterwards, with many additions

and changes. Yet here we have the spoken
rather than the written word; we can almost
hear the voice of the speaker, who thinks
aloud, and should be read aloud if all his
beauty is to be perceived. Words themselves
set him thinking and feeling; the momentum
of his mind presses through them and is
increased by them—is increased also, even to
us now as we read, by the presence of the
listening congregation. They had their part,
as with all great speakers, in the making of
these sermons, with their eager silence, their
expectant spirits. As the plays of Shakespeare
were made for the theatre, so was this eloquence
made for the church; and it is still quick with
that intercourse, not closet eloquence, but a
man speaking at one particular moment to
other men. If any speaker to-day would train
himself in eloquence, he could not do better
than to get some passages of Donne by heart;
not to imitate them, but because they have
the rhythm of speech, mastering thought
natural to the speaker and at one with it.
Often, even in the greatest passages, the
thought is obsolete to us; but the passion,
even the idea, lives through its past intellectual
forms. Donne, for instance, as in a famous
poem of his, takes the Resurrection of the

Body literally, almost ludicrously, but he rushes through his literal details to a close the more magnificent and surprising because of them.

In what corner, in what ventricle of the sea, lies all the jelly of a Body drowned in the *generall flood*? What coheerence, what sympathy, what dependence maintaines any relation, any correspondence, between that arm that was lost in Europe, and that leg that was lost in Afrique or Asia, scores of years between? One humour of our dead body produces worms, and those worms suck and exhaust all other humour, and then all dies, and all dries, and molders into dust, and that dust is blowen into the River, and that puddled water tumbled into the sea, and that ebs and flows in infinite revolutions, and still, still God knows in what cabinet every *seed-Pearle* lies, in what part of the world every grain of every mans dust lies; and, *sibilat populum suum*, (as his Prophet speaks in another case) he whispers, he hisses, he beckens, for the bodies of his Saints, and in the twinckling of an eye, that body that was scattered over all the elements, is sate down at the right hand of God, in a glorious resurrection.

There is a poem by Gerard Hopkins, Of the Comfort of the Resurrection, that seems to remember this passage, even to use Donne's method, though with another poet's freedom.

Donne's Sermons

At least there is, with the same theme, the same surprise in the close—

> Flesh fade, and mortal trash
> Fall to the residuary worm ; world's wildfire, leave
> but ash.
> In a flash, at a trumpet crash,
> I am at once what Christ is, since He was what I
> am, and
> This Jack, joke, poor potsherd, patch, matchwood,
> immortal diamond,
> Is immortal diamond.

Donne, too, has Hopkins's trick of letting one word call up another with its sound, a trick that would be tiresome if we could not almost hear him, in the silence of his congregation, making music and sense of his echoes.

When it comes to this height, that the fever is not in the humors, but in the spirits, that mine enemy is not an imaginary enemy, fortune, nor a transitory enemy, malice in great persons, but a reall, and an irresistible, and an inexorable, and an everlasting enemy, the Lord of Hosts himselfe, the Almighty God himselfe, the Almighty God himselfe onely knows the waight of this affliction, and except hee put in that *pondus gloriae*, that exceeding waight of an eternal glory, with his owne hand into the other scale, we are waighed downe, we are swallowed up, irreparably, irrevocably, irremediably.

There are passages of confession, as well as ecstasy, that remind us of Augustine—

I throwe myselfe downe in my Chamber, and I call in, and invite God, and his Angels thither, and when they are there, I neglect God and his Angels for the noise of a Flie, for the ratling of a Coach, for the whining of a doore; I take on in the same posture of praying; Eyes lifted up; knees bowed downe; as though I prayed to God; and, if God or his Angels should ask me, when I thought last of God in that prayer, I cannot tell. Sometimes I finde that I had forgot what I was about, but when I began to forget it, I cannot tell.

This honesty makes him humane even in his theology : " Never propose to thyself such a God, as thou wert not bound to imitate; thou mistakest God, if thou make him to be any such thing, or make him to do any such thing, as thou in thy proportions shouldst not do." The magnanimous man, such as Donne was, remains magnanimous even in his orthodoxy; he does indeed love his God and would not show Him unlovable. Nor, being a poet, would he lower men's spirits from his vantage-ground in the pulpit. "David proposes to himself, that he would sing of mercy, and of judgement; but it is of mercy first; and not of judgement at all otherwise than it will come into a song." It was the artist in him that freed him from the pedantries of imprecation; he knew they were ugly and that God does not love ugliness. Then, in a long passage, too long to be all quoted but short enough when read, he exalts his priesthood not in a vain professional pride but for a pretty, un-expected reason.

What a Coronation is our taking of orders, by which God makes us a Royall Priesthood. And what an inthronization is the coming up into a pulpit, where God invests His servants with His ordinance, as with a cloud, and then presses that cloud with a *Vae si non*, woe be unto thee, if thou doe not preach, and then enables him to preach peace, mercy, consolation to the whole congregation. That God should appear in a Cloud, upon the Mercy Seat, as He promises Moses He will doe, that from so poore a man as stands here, wrapped up in clouds of infirmity, and in clouds of iniquity, God should drop raine, poure down His dew, and sweeten that dew with His honey, and crust that honeyed dew into Manna, and multiply that Manna into Gomers, and fill those Gomers every day, and give every particular man his Gomer, give every soule in the congregation, consolation by me ;—

So it continues in a manner strange to us

now; but we know he is speaking the truth about himself, which a man must do if he is to persuade us that he speaks truth about God.

It is a misfortune that Donne never, except in a few short poems, found a form into which he could pour all his riches without any dross of pedantry. Mr. Pearsall Smith has made those extracts for us, because he was forced to make them for himself. Donne never was able to separate his fire from his smoke; and, the more you read him, the more you conjecture that he did not make the best of his life either. The God in him was frightened by the beast, that animal part of him which he cowed, but never transmuted utterly; it seems to growl in the pedantries of his prose, as earlier in the ugly fancies of his verse. He could not attain to the happy voluptuousness of one who sees heaven in all beauty; for him there was always the sting of lust and the curse of mortality in the flesh. So he longs always and never enjoys; longs for the unchanging, since change to him is full of danger; but there is the beauty of eternity itself in his longing for it, and here is prose that can be put beside the verse of Vaughan—

A day that hath no *pridie* or *postridie*, yesterday doth not usher it in, nor to-morrow

86

shall not drive it out. *Methusalem*, with all his hundreds of yeares, was but a Mushrome of a night's growth to this day. And all the foure Monarchies, with all their thousands of yeares, And all the powerfull Kings, and all the beautifull Queenes of this world, were but as a bed of flowers, some gathered at six, some at seaven, some at eight, All in one morning, in respect of this Day. In all the two thousand yeares of Nature, before the Law given by *Moses*, and the two thousand yeares of Law, before the Gospel given by Christ, and the two thousand yeares of Grace, which are running now, (of which last houre we have heard three quarters strike, more than fifteen hundred of this last two thousand spent) In all his six thousand, and in all those, which God may be pleased to adde, *In domo patris*, In this House of his Fathers, there was never heard quarter clock to strike, never seen minute glasse to turn.

Donne loved joy and longed for it; unlike many preachers, he preached it; rejoicing, he says, is the serenity of Heaven—

And he that hath not this joy here, lacks one of the best pieces of his evidence for the joyes of Heaven; and hath neglected or refused that Earnest by which God uses to bind his bargaine, that true joy in this world shall flow into the joy of Heaven as a river flows into the sea.

But here, too, and always, his beauty is the

beauty of longing; the voice almost breaks in
its song; he sows in tears, but he has not
yet reaped in joy. He loved " things extreme
and scattering bright," like the sun-lit rim of
a thunder-cloud; his beauty, like Dostoevsky's,
is wrung by faith out of anguish; and we can
understand how men crowded to witness that
passion, not as to a show, but that they might
share a life more intense, if more suffering, than
their own. For Donne must have lived in his
sermons as a musician in his music; men came
to see a wind shaken by the wind, by the wind
from an unknown country; they came to hear
words telling more than words can, and even
now they tell it to us. As Mr. Pearsall Smith
says—

It sometimes seems as if he were using time-
honoured phrases of the accepted faith, its hope
of Heaven, and its terror of the grave, to
express a vision of his own—a vision of life and
death, of evil and horror and ecstacy—very
different from that of other preachers; and we
are troubled as well as fascinated by the
strange music which he blows through the
sacred trumpets.

Yes, we are troubled, and it is a strange music,
in church, because other divines preach contentment, but Donne never. They see the universe

as a hierarchy, with every one, from God through the angels and saints and bishops and priests and deacons, down to the beggar, in his proper place. But for Donne, the poet, the artist, as for Christ Himself, humanity makes all men equal in desire for that Godhead and eternity and paradise which it is the aim of all to achieve. Platitudes about the insufficiency of this life were real to him; he valued in it only its hints and whispers of another. So he remained a wild poet like Poe even when he tried to speak the language of a dean; like Poe's, his mind was haunted with the thought of worms and corruption— "the conqueror worm" might be his phrase— because of his passion for an unchanging, untroubled eternity. In his last sermon he uses words to express the indignity of decay with an iteration almost mad:—

We must all pass this *posthume* death, this *death* after *death*, nay this death after buriall, this *dissolution* after *dissolution*, this *death* of *corruption* and *putrefaction*, of *vermiculation* and *incineration*, of *dissolution* and *dispersion* in and *from* the *grave*, when these bodies that have been the *children* of *royall parents*, and the *parents of royall children*, must say with *Job, Corruption, thou art my father*, and *to the Worm, thou art my mother and my sister*.

89

And, he ends, that we shall be—

mingled with the dust of every highway, and of every dung-hill, and swallowed in every puddle and pond. This is the most inglorious and contemptible *vilification*, the most deadly and peremptory *nullification* of man that we can consider.

Like Dürer's Melancolia, this is full of revolt and anguished disappointment after the glorification of man by the Renaissance. Raphael eternized the life of man here and now in his School at Athens; he painted triumphant minds thinking, untroubled, for ever. Dürer showed how thinking troubles the mind of man to madness, and Donne how these beautiful forms of the flesh must be wasted in corruption. He could never " forget to wonder that men are born to die "; he was half a Pagan, with a death's-head always at his feast, even at his feast of eloquence; but the other half of him staked all on the faith that his desires were true, that the will of God was his own deep, permanent will, and the bounty of God as infinite as his own expectation :—

He brought light out of darknesse, not out of a lesser light; he can bring thy Summer out of Winter, though thou have no Spring; though in the wayes of fortune, or understanding or conscience, thou have been benighted till now, wintred and frozen, clouded and eclypsed, damped and benummed, smothered and stupified till now, now God comes to thee, not as in the dawning of the day, not as in the bud of the spring, but as the Sun at noon to illustrate all shadowes, as the sheaves in harvest to fill all penuries, all occasions invite his mercies, and all times are his seasons.

The Brontës ✍ ✍ ✍ ✍ ✍

THE writings of the Brontës tempt one
to continual curiosity about their lives.
Villette and *Wuthering Heights* are wonderful
books, to be read for their own sakes; but they
are also events in a still more wonderful story,
the story of the Brontës. Everything written by
Charlotte seems to have some reference to her
life, to things which actually happened to her
and not merely to the inner experience of her
mind. So, when with this curiosity aroused
by her own words we read what is known
about her and discover the strangeness of her
life, we are tempted to find too much of her
actual experience in her novels. Miss Sinclair
seems to have written her *Three Brontës* to
warn us against this temptation. It is mainly
a commentary upon other books and contro-
versial throughout. We agree with much of
it, but we think that she would have done
better if she had forgotten the other books.

She is too protestant and above all too anxious
to prove that Charlotte was not a minx on the
look out for a husband. One might as well
defend St. Francis of Assisi against the charge
of other-worldliness. Minxes may have their
merits, but they live on a different level from
Charlotte Brontë. They have designs on
people ; she had a desire for a certain state
of being to which love was necessary, and for
that reason she desired love. Miss Sinclair,
in her anxiety to prove that she was no minx,
overlooks this desire of hers, and her Charlotte
is too negative. Indeed, in her enthusiasm for
Emily she sometimes writes of Charlotte like
an enemy. She speaks of Emily's superb
attitude to life, her detachment from the
stream of circumstance, and then tells us that
" Charlotte was at moments pitifully immersed
in the stream of circumstance, pitifully dependent on the material event." We are not
sure what she means, but we are sure that
Charlotte was never anything pitifully. And
here is a worse passage still :—

She had loved life, not as Emily loved it,
like an equal, with power over it and pride
and an unearthly understanding, virgin and
unafraid. There was something slightly subservient, consciously inferior, in Charlotte's
attitude to life. She had loved it secretly,

with a sort of shame, with a corroding passion and incredulity and despair. Such natures are not seldom victims of the power they would propitiate. It killed her in her effort to bring forth life.

As if there were any possible connexion between Charlotte's physical incapacity to bear a child and her philosophy or lack of it. With this kind of reasoning we might as well condemn *Wuthering Heights* because Emily died of comsumption and say that her stoicism was only the armour of a weakling. When once writers begin to talk about life as if it were a person they are sure to talk about human beings as if they were machines. The best part of Miss Sinclair's book is about Emily, and especially about her poems. She says some good things about Charlotte, but is inclined to make her a foil to Emily, a proceeding which Emily would have resented as much as anyone.

We have said that Charlotte had a desire for a certain state of being to which love was necessary. But Miss Sinclair insists rightly that she was not a sentimentalist. Indeed, if Charlotte was, or promised to be, the greatest English novelist of her time, it is because, besides being more strongly moved by experience than her rivals, she is free from that vice of sentimentality which weakened them. Dickens and Thackeray, with all their wider and larger experience, were apt to distort it for their own emotional pleasure or for the emotional pleasure of their readers. Charlotte Brontë is sometimes absurd from inexperience, but she never did that. She made up her mind early that life was hard, and that she could get from it very little of what she desired. She told herself that she was a plain woman who had to work for her living, and that her desires were not likely to alter the nature of the Universe. This, we suppose, is what Miss Sinclair means when she says that there was something slightly subservient and consciously inferior in her attitude towards life. Her mistake comes from thinking of life as a person. Towards real persons, towards men and women, Charlotte had the pride of Lucifer; and it was pride that kept her from being angry with things because they were not favourable to her desires. She was not subservient to life; but she would not lose her temper with it any more than she would lose her temper with a baby. When she moralizes, as she sometimes does, in a Sunday-school manner, it is not because such moralizing satisfies any part of her mind, but because she enjoys telling herself unpleasant facts. She never pretends to like the hardness of life or to think it just or reasonable; she only insists that it is hard and that it is no use to pretend otherwise.

And it is the same with people. In *Villette* she says of Paulina: "I liked her. It is not a declaration I have often made concerning my acquaintance in the course of this book; the reader will bear with it for once." Here there is a conscious revolt against what seemed to her the ordinary misrepresentations of fiction. She did not believe that there was as much affection in real life or as much reason for it as novels usually pretend. At any rate, people in her position did not find the world amiable, and she was not going to make any pretence of loving it so as to contrive a pretty story. The curious thing is that her proud submission to the hardness of life is more determined in *Villette*, written after the success of *Jane Eyre*, than in *Jane Eyre* itself. At the end of *Jane Eyre* she says: "I know what it is to live entirely for and with what I love best on earth. I hold myself supremely blest—blest beyond what language can express; because I am my husband's life as fully as he

is mine." Rochester even recovered the sight
of one eye and acknowledged that God had
tempered judgment with mercy. In *Villette*
there is neither mercy nor judgment but
the chance of a storm, the issue of which
the reader can take to be what he chooses.
"Leave sunny imaginations hope," says the
writer, and we know that her own imagination
is not sunny. "Madame Beck prospered all
the days of her life; so did Père Silas.
Madame Walravens fulfilled her ninetieth
year before she died." There is a happy ending for you if you want it, thrown like a bone
to a dog. Charlotte Brontë does not believe
that happiness comes to those who know best
what happiness might be. She does not for a
moment believe that Lucy Snowe could have
had with Doctor John that kind of happiness
which the Jane Eyre of the past had enjoyed
with Rochester. Doctor John throughout
Villette is treated as a day-dream. If he
begins to be the hero of the book, it is only
to show that heroes are not for Lucy Snowe,
however much she may have dreamed of them.
And soon she seems to console herself with
the thought that heroes are heroes only to
heroines. That, I think, is the real reason
why Doctor John is a failure, and not because,

as Miss Sinclair says, Charlotte is too consciously preoccupied with him. She had never
met a man who seemed to her like the hero of
a novel, and when she tried to draw one she
was hampered by scepticism. She keeps telling
herself that Doctor John is ordinary, though
good. He would no doubt seem a hero to a
woman' who fell in love with him ; but Lucy
Snowe, like her creator, was not the woman to
indulge herself in a hopeless passion. Throughout *Villette* Charlotte revolts against Doctor
John and against the convention that would
make him the chief character in it. She is for
the men and women who do not get happiness
so easily ; and they triumph in her masterpiece,
not materially, but because their griefs and
joys interest us more than any mechanically
contrived happiness of heroes and heroines.

But though Lucy Snowe is plain and quiet,
and though M. Emanuel can make himself
ridiculous, they both have the genius of their
creator. Charlotte Brontë, though she despised the heroes and heroines of circumstance,
worshipped genius, and was, perhaps, the only
English novelist who could represent it, not by
telling us about the wonders it achieves, but
by revealing its mind to us. Lucy Snowe and
Paul Emanuel do no wonders; but in them

she shows us genius without its works ; and in her description of Rachel she no longer tries to conceal her worship. Rachel did not know that the one woman in Europe of a genius equal to her own, and greater, was watching her; and that woman an English Miss whom none of her own admirers would have looked at twice, a little Puritan who knew nothing of the world except by intuition, who hated the Pope, despised foreigners, and was ready to believe all actresses wicked. She had been told that Rachel was not good, she says—

Wicked, perhaps, she is, but also she is strong; and her strength has conquered beauty, has overcome grace, and bound both at her side, captives peerlessly fair, and docile as fair. . . . Fallen, insurgent, banished, she remembers the heaven where she rebelled. Heaven's light, following her exile, pierces its confines, and discloses its forlorn remoteness.

And then at the end, in her delight of understanding another genius with her own, she forgets all about the rumoured wickedness :—

I had seen acting before, but never anything like this—never anything which astonished Hope and hushed Desire; which outstripped Impulse and paled Conception; which, instead of merely irritating imagination with the thought of what might be done, at the same time fevering the nerves because it was not done, disclosed power like a deep, swollen winter river thundering in cataract, and bearing the soul, like a leaf, on the steep and steely sweep of its descent.

Like another Puritan, she is carried away by her Lucifer and reveals herself and her own rebellion in her description of Rachel's. It was not merely common inadequate art but common inadequate life also which irritated her imagination with the thought of what might be done, at the same time fevering the nerves because it was not done; and in all her books there is the conflict between her desires and her determination not to mistake reality. She had those thoughts which wander through eternity; she had her own conception of a heaven which she would not give up for any conventional idea of happiness and by which she measured all earthly things and people. But what made her and her art remarkable was her determination not to lose herself in dreams of that heaven, not to exchange ugly truth for any pretty illusion. We wonder that she should have come out of that Yorkshire parsonage, as if she wrote by a miracle about things she had never seen or known. But it was the contrast between her

real life and what she desired that made her
art. Everything good in it is taken from
external or internal experience; there is the
dark foil of reality to all her dreams. She is
the most lyrical of our novelists, because everything that happened to her moved her to
emotion through the contrast between what
was and what she desired. The plot is always
made by the adventures of her own soul, and
they are stranger than any adventures of
romantic heroes in outlandish countries.
When first *Jane Eyre* appeared there was
resentment both of men and of women that a
woman should speak so frankly of the adventures of her soul. The world was used to a
Rachel telling everything about herself and
women on the stage; it was not used to an
English governess, the daughter of a country
parson, making the same revelations with more
frankness and greater power. It was lawful
for a woman to describe how women acted and
spoke when in love with men; it was not
lawful for her to expose the mind of a woman
who was in love with love itself. We enjoy the
dreams of young men about love, especially
in lyrical poetry ; but here was a girl who,
with primeval innocence, not merely expressed
her dreams in poetry but represented them in

fiction, showing the woman who dreamed them so vividly that every one knew she was real. Hence the *Quarterly* reviewer, he or she, was determined to believe either that she was not real or that she was not a fair specimen of her kind; a man must have written the book, or, if not a man, a woman who, for some reason, had long forfeited the society of her own sex.

That reviewer knew nothing of the other side of Charlotte Brontë, the bravery that went with her innocence; and he or she was as far out as the reviewer who conjectured that *In Memoriam* must have been written by the widow of a military man. Charlotte Brontë remarks that when the world was younger and haler than now moral trials were a deeper mystery still. "Perhaps in all the land of Israel there was but one Saul—certainly but one David to soothe or comprehend him." So when she wrote women were a deeper mystery even than they are now; the idea that they should tell the secrets of their own hearts, or had any secrets to tell, had not existed, perhaps, since the time of Sappho. Perhaps in the whole of England there was but one Charlotte Brontë, certainly but one Emily to comprehend her. It was the Brontë family that made each of them write with that

wonderful frankness and innocence. There
were two girls, if not three, who knew the
secrets of each other's hearts and knew where
their own were safe from misunderstanding.
Their dreadful home was their fortress against
the world, to which they returned to renew
their strength in communion with each other.
For Emily it was the world; and everything
outside was a nightmare of unreality. In
Wuthering Heights we seem to see her mind
lost in that nightmare and fighting with
it, but never losing courage. So she fought
with death itself; and for Charlotte the
memory of her death and the others made the
outside world always lonely and inhospitable.
"The spirit was inexorable to the flesh," she
said of Emily after she was dead. She herself
could make terms with the world, but they
were her own terms. She conquered it, and
cared so little for her conquest that she
married her father's curate, not having found
either Rochester or Paul Emanuel in real life.
We must not suppose that she took him
because she could find no one better. That
would be a gross misunderstanding. She loved
him as much as she could love any reality; but
it was only by the conquest of herself that she
was able to love an ordinary man at all.

Dostoevsky ∾ ∾ ∾ ∾ ∾

THE novels of Dostoevsky discover a strange world to us, in which people talk and act like no one that we have ever met, yet we do not read them because we wish to hear about these strange Russian people, so unlike ourselves. Rather we read them because they remind us of what we had forgotten about ourselves, as a scent may suddenly remind us of some place or scene not remembered since childhood. And as we have no doubt about the truth of the memories recalled by a scent, so we have none about Dostoevsky's truth. It is strange like those memories of childhood, but only because it has been so long sleeping in our minds. He has no need to prove it; he presents it for our recognition, and we recognize it at once, however contrary it may be to all that we are accustomed to believe about ourselves.

The strangeness of Dostoevsky's novels lies in his method, which is unlike that of other novelists because his interest is different from theirs. The novel of pure plot is all concerned

with success or failure; the hero has some task
to perform, and we read to discover whether
he succeeds in performing it. But even in
novels where character is more considered it is
still the interest of failure and success which
usually makes the plot. The hero, for instance,
falls in love, and the plot forms round this
love; or he is married, and there is a suspense
about his happiness or unhappiness. But in
the greatest of Dostoevsky's books, such as
The Brothers Karamazov or *The Idiot*, the
interest is not in the happiness or unhappiness of the hero; for to Dostoevsky
happiness and unhappiness are external things,
and he is not concerned even with this kind of
failure or success. He has so firm a belief in
the existence of the soul, and with it a faith so
strong in the order of the universe, that he
applies no final tests whatever to this life.
Plot with most novelists is an effort to make
life seem more conclusive than it is; and that
is one of the reasons why we like a firm plot in
a novel. With its tests and judgments and
results it produces an illusion of certainty
agreeable to our weakness of faith; but
Dostoevsky needs no illusion of certainty, and
gives none. He had a faith independent of
happiness and even of the state of his own

soul. Life had poured unhappiness upon him so that he knew the worst of it from his own experience; yet we can tell from his books that he knew also a peace of thought compared with which his own miseries were unreal to him. In that he differs from Tolstoy, who saw this peace of thought in the distance and could not reach it. Tolstoy therefore conceived of life as an inevitable discord between will and conviction, and tried to impose the impossible on mankind as he tried to impose it upon himself, judging them with the severity of his self-judgments. His books are full of his own pursuit of certainty and his own half-failure and half-success. He still makes happiness the test, even though he knows that the noblest of men cannot attain to it; for his own unhappiness was caused by the conflict in his mind between will and conviction. But in Dostoevsky this conflict had ceased. He was not happy, but he was not torn by the desire for happiness; nor did he test his own soul or the souls of others by their happiness. His faith in the soul was so great that he saw it independent of circumstance, almost independent of its own manifestations in action. For in these manifestations there is always the alloy of circumstance, of the passions of the

Dostoevsky

flesh, or of good or evil fortune; and he tried
to see the soul free of this. He did not judge
men by the diversities which outward things
seem to impose on them; for him the soul was
more real than all these diversities, and they
only interested him for their power of revealing
or obscuring it. Therefore his object in his
novels is to reveal the soul, not to pass any
judgments upon men nor to tell us how they
fare in this world; and this object makes his
peculiar method. He does not try to show us
souls free from their bodies or from circumstance, for to do that would be contrary to
his own experience and his own faith. Rather
he shows them tormented and mistranslated,
even to themselves, but in such a way that we
see the reality beyond the torments and the
mistranslations. His characters drift together
and fall into long wayward conversations that
have nothing to do with any events in the
book. They quarrel about nothing; they have
no sense of shame; they behave intolerably, so
that we know we should hate them in real
life. But, as we read, we do not hate them,
for we recognize ourselves—not indeed in their
words and behaviour, but in what they reveal
through these. They have an extreme frankness which may be in the Russian character

but which is also part of Dostoevsky's method, for the characters of other Russian novelists are not so frank as his. He makes them talk and act so as to reveal themselves, and for no other purpose whatever. Yet they reveal themselves unconsciously, and their frankness, though surprising, is not incredible.

But we, accustomed to novels concerned with failure and success, and with plots formed upon that concern, are bewildered by Dostoevsky's method; and even he is a little bewildered by it. He never quite learned how to tell his own kind of story, a story in which all outward events are subordinate to the changes and manifestations of the soul. Even in *The Brothers Karamazov* there is a plot, made out of the murder of old Karamazov, which seems to be imposed upon the real interest of the book as the unintelligible plot of *Little Dorrit* is imposed upon the real interest of that masterpiece. And in *The Idiot* events are so causeless and have so little effect that we cannot remember them. The best plan is not to try to remember them, for they matter very little; the book is about the souls of men and women, and where the construction is clumsy it is only because Dostoevsky is impatient to tell us what he has to tell.

Dostoevsky

Those who believe that the soul is only an illusion—and there are many who believe this without knowing it—will be surprised to find how much truth Dostoevsky has discovered through his error. Whether his faith was right or wrong, it certainly served him well as a novelist, and so did his experience. No modern writer has been so well acquainted with evil and misery as he was. Other novelists write about them as moving exceptions in life; he wrote about them because, in his experience, they were the rule. Other novelists write about them because they have a quarrel with life or with society, or with particular institutions; but he has no quarrel with anything; there is neither hatred in him, nor righteous indignation, nor despair. He had suffered from Government as much as any man in the world, yet he never saw it as a hideous abstraction, and its crimes and errors were for him only the crimes and errors of men like himself.

We hate men when they seem no longer men to us, when we see nothing in them but tendencies which we abhor; and a novelist who expresses his hatred of tendencies in his characters deprives them of life and makes them uninteresting to all except those who share his hatred. Even Tolstoy makes some of his characters lifeless through hatred; but Dostoevsky hates no one, for behind every tendency he looks for the soul, and the tendency only interests him because of the soul that is concealed or betrayed by it. Thus his wicked people, and they abound, are never introduced into his books either to gratify his hatred of them or to make a plot with their wickedness. He is as much concerned with their souls as with the souls of his saints, Alyosha and Prince Myshkin. Iago seems to be drawn from life, but only from external observation; we never feel that Shakespeare has been Iago himself, or has deduced him from possibilities in himself. But Dostoevsky's worst characters are like Hamlet. He knows things about them that he could only know about himself, and they live through his sympathy, not merely through his observation. He makes no division of men into sheep and goats—not even that subtle division, common in the best novels, by which the sheep are more real than the goats. For him all men have more likeness to each other than unlikeness, for they all have souls; and because he is always aware of the soul in them he has a Christian sense of their equality. It is not merely rich and poor or clever or stupid

that are equal to him, but even good and bad.
He treats the drunkard Lebedyev with respect,
and, though his books contain characters as
absurd as any in Dickens, he does not intro-
duce them, like Dickens, to make fun of them,
but because he is interested in the manner
in which their absurdities mistranslate them.
Nor is the soul made different for him by sex,
for that is only a difference of the body. So he
does not insist on femininity in his women; he
knows them, but he knows them as human
beings like men ; and he is interested in sexual
facts not as they affect his own passions but
as they affect the soul. He, like his hero
Myshkin, was an epileptic, and what he tells
us of Myshkin's attitude towards women may
have been true of himself. But if that is so,
his own lack of appetite, like the deafness of
Beethoven, made his art more profound and
spiritual; he makes no appeal to the passions
of his readers, as Beethoven in his later works
makes none to the mere sense of sound.

He was an artist purified by suffering as
saints are purified by it; for through it he
attained to that complete disinterestedness
which is as necessary to the artist as to the
saint. Whenever a man sees people and
things in relation only to his own personal

wants and appetites he cannot use them as subject-matter for art. Dostoevsky learnt to free everything and everybody from this relation more completely, perhaps, than any writer known to us. Not even vanity or fear, nor any theory begotten of them, perverted his view of human life. In his art at any rate he achieved that complete liberation which is aimed at by the wisdom of the East; and his heroes exhibit it in their conduct. Myshkin would be a man of no account in our world, but Christ might have chosen him for one of his Apostles; any Western novelist, drawing such a character, would have made him unreal by insisting upon his goodness and by displaying it only in external actions, as saints in most European pictures are to be recognized only by a halo and a look of silly sanctity. We fail with such characters because we should not recognize them if we met them in real life, and because we do not even wish to be like them ourselves. They represent an ideal imposed on us long ago from the East, and now only faintly and conventionally remembered. We test everybody by some kind of success in this life, even if it be only the success of a just self-satisfaction. But Myshkin has not even that; he is unconscious of his own goodness, and of

the badness of other men. People who meet
him are impatient with him and call him " the
idiot " because he seems to be purposeless and
defenceless; but we do not feel that the
novelist has afflicted them with incredible
blindness, for we know, as we read, that we too
should call Myshkin an idiot if we met him.
His understanding has never been trained by
competition or defence, but that is the reason
why now and then it surprises every one by its
profundity; for he understands men's minds
because, like Dostoevsky himself, he does not
see them in relation to his own wants, and
because his disinterestedness makes them put
off all disguise before him.

" Dear Prince," some one says to him, " it's
not easy to reach paradise on earth; but you
reckon on finding it. Paradise is a difficult
matter, Prince—much more difficult than it
seems to your good heart." But Myshkin's
heart is not good because it cherishes illusions;
he does not expect to find paradise on earth,
and he does not like people because he thinks
them better than they are. Seeing clearly
what they are, he likes even the worst of them
in spite of it; and to read Dostoevsky's books
throws us for the time into Myshkin's state of
mind. When we are confronted with some

fearful wickedness, even when we read about it in the newspapers, it shakes our faith in life and makes it seem a nightmare in which ordinary comfortable reality has suddenly turned into horror. But in Dostoevsky's books the horror of the nightmare suddenly turns to a happy familiar beauty. He shows us wickedness worse than any we had ever imagined, wickedness which, if we met with it in real life, would make us believe in human monsters without souls; and then, like music rising through the discord of madness, he shows us a soul, like our own, behind that wickedness. And we believe in the one as we have believed in the other; for we feel that a man is telling us about life who has ceased to fear it, and that his faith, tested by the suffering which he reveals in his books, is more to be trusted than our own experience.

The Promise of Keats

M R. BRIDGES' essay on Keats was written more than twenty years ago, and he has since revised it. It is one of the best essays in our language upon a great poet, or, rather, upon his poetry ; for Mr. Bridges shows little psychological curiosity about Keats in it. He gives us an analysis of Endymion which should be read by every one who wishes to enjoy that work. About all the poems of which he speaks he has something simple and true and precise to say ; yet I am not satisfied. Or, rather, I wish to add something to what he has said and to differ a little from what he implies, if not from what he asserts.

Keats, he says at the beginning of his essay, " was smitten down in his youth, in the very maturing of his powers, which, having already produced work of almost unrivalled beauty, held a promise of incredible things." There I both agree and dissent. I do not believe

that Keats died in the very maturing of his
powers. Rather, when he was overcome by
disease, there was a change working in him
which made him a beginner again; and in this
change was the promise of incredible things.
He was the prize student among English poets,
though he won no prize in his lifetime. No
one ever did such student work as Hyperion;
and he did not finish it because it was student
work. It even gave him a disgust of his
master, Milton. Mr. Bridges quotes him on
this point. "I have but lately stood on my
guard against Milton. Life to him would be
death to me." Even in the great Odes there
are marks of the student, passages of delighted
virtuosity that remind one of the student
drawings of Mr. John. In the Ode to the
Nightingale he is further from natural speech
than Shelley in his best lyrics; he is producing
a splendid work of art and enjoying the sense
that he is doing so.

To cease upon the midnight with no pain.

That is the phrase of a wonderful student; but
Shelley wrote poetry more naturally than he
wrote a letter; and Keats did not understand
or admire this freedom of his. He thought
that Shelley did not pay enough respect to

The Promise of Keats

poetry and told him to curb his magnanimity, be more of an artist, and load every rift with ore. Those are modern words; they might have been said by an art student of to-day; and Keats is the first modern art student known to us. That, no doubt, was why he irritated not only dull, peevish men like Gifford, but also men of the world like Byron. He seemed to them a narrow little, impudent Cockney; and he had the modern impudence and frivolity of manner, the modern eagerness for all kinds of ideas and audacity in expressing them. He was at home with ideas long before he was at home with people; one can imagine him, now, in a studio in Chelsea, slipshod and restless, shy yet talkative, and with a cigarette always loosely held between his lips. So he has been the favourite poet of art students and of clever young poets who are learning their craft. He writes as they would like to write; they see how magnificently he brings things off, how there is the scent of poetry itself in the " magic casements," and " the large utterance of the early gods," and " the music yearning like a god in pain," and " the besieging wind's uproar." It is of such phrases that the young poet dreams; they are poetry to him; and he who can make them lives a life

that is worth living. Keats thought that
himself; words were to him a delicious material;
and he seems to feel them with delicate fingers,
to give them quality with his touch as Chardin
gave quality to paint. All that feeling is expressed consciously in his fragment of an Ode
to Maia :—

> Mother of Hermes ! and still youthful Maia !
>   May I sing to thee
> As thou wast hymned on the shores of Baiae?
>   Or may I woo thee
> In earlier Sicilian? or thy smiles
> Seek as they once were sought, in Grecian isles,
> By bards who died content on pleasant sward,
> Leaving great verse unto a little clan?
> O, give me their old vigour, and unheard
> Save of the quiet primrose, and the span
>   Of heaven and few ears,
> Rounded by thee, my song should die away
>   Content as theirs,
> Rich in the simple worship of a day.

It is rounded like a piece on the violin played
by a master, and the delight of rounding it
seemed then to Keats the best thing in life.

Because he did this wonderful student work
we are apt to think of him as one whose career
was determined. He means to us the Ode to
the Nightingale and odes unwritten of the
same kind. His furthest point of progress is
La belle dame sans merci or the fragment of

The Promise of Keats

The Eve of St. Mark; and who could go further than that? Yet these are not his furthest point of progress, and it is not they that hold the promise of incredible things. He could not have done better that way; but he was starting on a different way foreshadowed in The Fall of Hyperion. Many things led him into it; already in 1818 he had said that he would turn all his soul to the love of philosophy; and one can see in his letters how strong this love was in him. There is no opposition, as Mr. Bridges points out, " between his true instinct for ideal philosophy and his luxurious poetry (which seems rather its young expression)," and for a time he sought a philosophical justification for that luxurious poetry. But philosophy made him think about his art, made him desire to enrich it with the whole of himself. There came a time when it seemed to him that in his romantic poetry he was playing a game; and in the Fall of Hyperion he expresses the same mood that is expressed by the young Shakespeare at the end of *Love's Labour's Lost*. The Veiled Shadow says to him :—

>   Thou hast felt
> What 'tis to die and live again before
> Thy fated hour; that thou hadst power to do so
> Is thine own safety.

This is the language of conversion, and the Shadow proceeds to tell him how he can attain to salvation both in life and in art—

" None can usurp this height," returned that shade,
" But those to whom the miseries of the world
Are misery, and will not let them rest.
All else who find a haven in the world,
Where they may thoughtless sleep away their days,
If by a chance into this fane they come,
Rot on the pavement where thou rottedst half.

That is to say the poet, the artist, who sees in life nothing but material for his art, ceases to be even a poet, an artist, repeats his own youth when he is past it, and rots away in the haven he has made for himself. The dreamer and the poet are distinct—

Diverse, sheer opposite, antipodes,
The one pours out a balm upon the world,
Theother vexes it.

So his masterpieces seemed to Keats mere dreaming. He had half unconsciously expressed in them moods simpler than he actually experienced, moods which he assumed so that he might simplify the problems of his difficult art. Now he was no longer content to do so; his desire was to write poetry with all his faculties and to enrich it with all his experience, whether that seemed poetical in itself or prosaic.

The Promise of Keats

It is strange how classical and romantic mean the same error when they express a defect of art. They mean a refusal of experience so that art may be made easy, as if the essence of art were the choice of experience and not the transfiguration of it. Keats saw that, as a romantic poet, he had been fastidiously choosing experience, and that at two removes. He had dreamed about the past as something that he could experience æsthetically. He sees the figures on a Grecian Urn removed out of time, freed from anxiety and mischance—

Fair Youth, beneath the trees, thou canst not leave
   Thy song, nor ever can those trees be bare;
     Bold Lover, never, never canst thou kiss,
Though winning near the goal—yet, do not grieve;
     She cannot fade, though thou hast not thy
       bliss,
   For ever wilt thou love, and she be fair.

When he wrote this he envied this perfect unreality—it seemed to him better than haphazard hand-to-mouth reality, as all art seemed to him better than life; and he would turn away from the present to the beautiful dumb-show of the past that he could watch from a distance, to lovers who did nothing but love and for whom love was all passionate gestures.

Between him and the subject-matter of his art
there was a gulf like that between the audience
and the stage, and he did not look at the rest
of the audience. His eyes were fixed upon
those figures of passion who had no life outside
their passion, and whose passion therefore was
itself unreal. He tried to live himself in their
heaven, which was not a heaven of pure joy,
but of detachment from the struggle for life
and from all ideas connected with it.

Mr. Bridges points out how in the Epistle
to John Hamilton Reynolds Keats rebels
against the ideas which the struggle for life
fosters in the mind of man. He wishes to see
the beauty of the visible world simply, and to
have his ideas controlled by it, as if they were
dreams caused by circumstances—

> O that our dreamings all, of sleep or wake,
> Would all their colours from the sunset take :
> From something of material sublime,
> Rather than shadow our own soul's day-time
> In the dark void of night.

He wished to be passive to beauty, even if it
were unmeaning, rather than active in his own
version of life as it happened to him ; and that
is the romantic attitude always.

But he discovered that, while he had been
watching love and writing of it thus in the

The Promise of Keats

past, he did not know what love was. Mr. Bridges speaks of his failure in the delineation of human passion and charges him with a lack of true insight into it, " which may have been due to the absence of awakening experience." He speaks, too, of his superficial and unworthy treatment of his ideal female characters. It is true that they are apt to be " pusses," Cockney young ladies whom one might take for an outing; and Keats himself fell in love with a " puss." But, having done so, he discovered what love really was—not a matter of gestures and music, not something that transported him from the audience on to the stage, but something that troubled the whole of his body and soul. It was not a duet in which the perfect concord, whether of sorrow or joy, overcame all irrelevant facts; rather, it kept all the imperfection, misgiving, and discord of reality and heightened them. He found that by the mere process of loving he could not pass into the world of the Eve of St. Agnes; there were still two separate human beings, and the other was not ready to sing the part he had dreamed for her.

Out of this discovery he made strange poetry, poetry that has in it the promise of incredible things. In the Ode to Fanny and the Lines to Fanny he shows us that he was indeed awakened by experience, frightened by a love that began to seem, not freedom, but slavery. He saw that he was surrendering himself to another, and that other not purely a lover but herself, untransfigured by love. He saw the slave not of an angel of romance, but of a woman with all the haphazard, unredeemed prose of life still in her. Fanny Brawne was an individual, not a type; but he was still bound to her, and to the hard facts in her that he could not love for themselves. In the Ode to Fanny he is tormented by jealousy. He knows that she is a minx, and she is going to a dance without him, where she will flirt; there are all the trivial ignominies of infatuation, yet he transforms them in his poetry—

Who now, with greedy looks, eats up my feast?
What stare outfaces now my silver moon?
Ah, keep that hand unravish'd at the least;
    Let, let the amorous burn—
    But, pry'thee, do not turn
The current of your heart from me so soon.
    O! save, in charity,
    The quickest pulse for me.

And the poem ends with the desperate serious-

ness of a passion that he knows will not be
understood—

> Ah ! if you prize my subdued soul above
> The poor, the fading, brief pride of an hour ;
> Let none profane my Holy See of love,   '
>   Or with a rude hand break
>   The sacramental cake ;
> Let none else touch the just new-budded flower :
>   If not—may my eyes close,
>   Love ! on their last repose.

But still stranger, and with still more
promise of incredible' things, are the Lines to
Fanny, in which we see him possessed by the
fear of love ; almost hating it, though he
cannot hate her, because he knows that love
will persist and yet be subdued to the discords,
the imperfections, the routine of life ; that it
can continue when the morning freshness and
the music are gone from it—

> Where shall I learn to get my peace again ?
> To banish thoughts of that most hateful land,
> Dungeoner of my friends, that wicked strand
> Where they were wreck'd and live a wrecked life ;
> That monstrous region, where dull rivers pour,
> Ever from their sordid urns unto the shore,
> Unown'd of any weedy-haired gods ;
> Whose winds, all zephyrless, hold scourging rods,
> Iced in the great lakes, to afflict mankind ;
> Whose rank-grown forests, frosted, black, and blind,

Would fright a Dryad ; whose harsh-herbaged meads
Make lean and lank the starv'd ox while he feeds ;
There bad flowers have no scent, birds no sweet
    song,
And great unerring Nature once seems wrong.

It is the awakening of La belle dame sans merci expressed with a new psychological precision ; and it seems to promise that Keats was to be the Donne of the romantic movement, but a greater Donne who had mastered that which he forsook, who could express his disillusionment with all the music of his old illusions.

But always he returns from these rebellions and misgivings with a sick passion to the hope of a complete rest and harmony in love—

I cry your mercy—pity—love !—aye, love !
    Merciful love that tantalises not,
One-thoughted, never-wandering, guileless love,
    Unmask'd, and being seen—without a blot !

This Fanny Brawne could not give him ; she was not ready to play her part as the mistress of a poet. Keats was to her just her young man whom she would play off against other young men ; yet he was bound to her by the sick, exasperated desire of the consumptive. He longed to be free, to feel and think about the universe, and he could feel and think about her alone. A little longer and he might have written of her as Catullus wrote of Lesbia ; but he went to Italy to die and, on the way, wrote that last sonnet in which he still dreamt of a Nirvana of love.

Nothing could be sadder than this last return to an impossible dream, and the thought that he left her, baffled and starving, with no other dream to take its place. But we are concerned now with that last growth of his mind which was stopped in its first promise by disease. Nothing foreshadows his unguessed greatness so much as this power of writing a strange new poetry about his first discomforting experience of passion. He might have thrust it to the back of his mind and refused to write poetry about it ; he might have remained a forlorn romantic without conviction. But he was too great a poet not to accept the experience in all its ugliness and sharpness. To him the miseries of the world were at last misery and not something to make poetry about. He saw the general unhappiness in his own ; he saw that reality alone was interesting, however disconcerting it might be ; and that it was reality only to those who experienced it fully. There is fullness of experience in those Lines to Fanny as in no earlier poem of his yet it is all poetized. He can make phrases about it as rich as any he made about the nightingale—

And great unerring nature once seems wrong.

Perhaps that is the finest line he ever wrote; more than any other, at least, it promises the incredible things that he would have written. It is strange that Shelley, who cared for little of his poetry, who cannot have known that his mind was like the wide world dreaming of things to come, should yet have given a convincing music to our dreams about him—

It was for thee yon kingless sphere has long
Swung blind in unascended majesty,
Silent alone amid an Heaven of Song.
Assume thy winged throne, thou Vesper of our
    throng.

We cannot believe that such a mind shared the corruption of the body, that such a music ended, broken and dismayed by its own ending. Shelley knew, when he was among the prophets, that—

The soul of Adonais, like a star,
Beacons from the abode where the Eternal are.

The Note-Books of Samuel Butler ᢨ

SAMUEL BUTLER said that "the true writer will stop everywhere and anywhere to put down his notes, as the true painter will stop everywhere and anywhere to sketch." He himself, as Mr. Festing Jones tells us in his preface to The Note-Books, began to make notes early, and continued until he died. For the last eleven years of his life he spent an hour a day re-editing them; and he left five bound volumes of them, with enough material unbound to make another volume. Mr. Festing Jones has made selections from all these, grouping the notes under different heads; and he has added an index which I have tested and found excellent. For the first enjoyment of the book all that is needed is to read it through; but afterwards anyone who deserves to possess it will want to know his way about it. The index will guide him; and the editor deserves our thanks for that almost as much as for giving us the book itself.

Samuel Butler was a born writer, but also a born amateur. He knew this himself, and he was no doubt thinking of his own work when he wrote a note upon Amateurs and Professionals.

There is no excuse [he says] for amateur work being bad. Amateurs often excuse their shortcomings on the ground that they are not professionals, the professional could plead with greater justice that he is not an amateur. . . . He has got to square every one all round, and will assuredly fail to make his way unless he does this; if, then, he betrays his trust he does so under temptation. . . .

The question is, what is the amateur an amateur of ? What is he really in love with ? Is he in love with other people, thinking he sees something which he would like to show them ? . . . If this is his position he can do no wrong, the spirit in which he works will ensure that his defects will be only as bad spelling or bad grammar in some pretty saying of a child.

In fact, the amateur can afford to be disinterested ; and Butler ordered his whole life so that he might be able to afford this expensive luxury. Not only did he learn to do with very little money ; he also economized in beliefs and emotions, not because he was by nature cold or sceptical, but because he would not be a partisan of any one view of life. He seems to have regarded himself as a consecrated bachelor; Melchisedec, he says, was a really happy man. "He was without father, without mother, and without descent. He was an incarnate bachelor. He was a born orphan." He wished to be a Melchisedec free from all ties whatever, spiritual and intellectual as well as material. He only wrote a book, he said, when it came to him and insisted upon being written, and it was the same with convictions. He did not seek after them, they had to force themselves upon him. Such a man would be an uninteresting failure if he had no convictions; Butler is interesting because his convictions, though few, were strong.

He had, as he takes pains to show us, no grievance against life or the human race. If a sentimentalist had complained that nothing was sacred to him he might have answered that everything was sacred. That was the reason why he was ready to joke about everything he made no division between sheep and goats, between the serious and the trivial, between the sublime and the ridiculous. He was at ease about the universe as much as a mediæval Christian about his religion, and had the same delight in profanity. The Note-books are full of his naughtiness; and no one could be shocked by it who did not enjoy being shocked. "It is all very well for mischievous writers to maintain that we cannot serve God and Mammon. Granted that it is not easy, but nothing that is worth doing ever is easy." That remark is worth considering, because Butler had no personal interest in making it. He was not trying to excuse himself for serving Mammon alone; he had an indifference to Mammon so complete that he could say a good word for him. So Keats told Shelley that an artist must serve Mammon. "He must have self-concentration—selfishness perhaps." Both mean that there is always a practical problem to be solved; and Butler would have said that, as God sets the problem, you cannot serve Him without serving Mammon.

Butler's naughtiness is an indulgence that he permits himself, knowing that it will not become a vice of his mind. It was as delicious to him as idleness to a busy man—and as necessary. For his weakness was to become too serious about everything that he undertook; he enjoyed the game of proving just as much as the game of disproving, and he convinced himself that Nausicaa wrote the Odyssey. Indeed, but for his recreations of naughtiness, he might have become a bigot or at least a crank. It

was his instinct of self-preservation that drove
him to them; and in them he reacted against
himself as much as against anyone else.
Swift, incessant reaction is the secret of
Butler's wit; it was what gave life to his
thought and adventures to his mind. With
some comic writers it is a vulgar trick played
coldly and mechanically. With Butler it is a
habit, but a habit that surprises even him; and
we feel the surprise in his unexpected turns of
speech. It is a reaction, too, just as often from
the absurd to the serious as from the serious to
the absurd. Take, for instance, this passage
headed "Night-shirts and Babies," which
affords a good example of the adventures of
his mind :—

On Hindhead, last Easter, we saw a family
wash hung out to dry. There were papa's
two great night-shirts and mamma's two lesser
nightgowns, and then the children's smaller
articles of clothing and mamma's drawers and
the girls' drawers, all full swollen with a strong
north-east wind. But mamma's nightgown
was not so well pinned on, and, instead of being
full of steady wind, like the others, kept blow-
ing up and down as though she were preaching
wildly. . . . I should like a *Santa Famiglia*
with clothes drying in the background.

That desire for a Holy Family with clothes

drying in the background expresses the whole character of Butler's mind. It was not that he wanted to sneer at the Holy Family, but that he liked the beautiful and the comic in the same picture. His mind got zest for each from the contrast between them; he was like the builders of the Middle Ages, who adorned their cathedrals with gargoyles, and he liked to play the part of a gargoyle himself, grinning among all the solemnities of the universe yet not incongruous with them. It is the glory of Gothic art that it has room for the grotesque as well as the beautiful; and for Butler life itself had the same glory. He made his jests about everything in heaven and earth, not because he thought nothing serious, but because he tested the seriousness of everything by its power to survive the ordeal. No one ever had more of the humorist's delight in the universal imperfection of things. "All progress," he said, "is based upon a universal, innate desire on the part of every organism to live beyond its income." He laughed, as M. Bergson says we always laugh, at the victory of the mechanical over life; but this very laughter implied, as all genuine laughter must, the belief that life is not mechanical. "Life," he says, "is eight parts cards and two parts play, the unseen world is made manifest to us in the play." There was nothing he hated so much as heresies of perfection in morals, science, or art; he hated any explanation of anything that professed to be complete, any ambition of absolute virtue, any attempt to produce perfect beauty; and that not because he disbelieved in truth, virtue, and beauty, for he loved them all three, but because he thought they could only manifest themselves in imperfection. Of the philosopher he says:—

He should have made many mistakes and been saved often by the skin of his teeth, for the skin of one's teeth is the most teaching thing about one. He should have been, or at any rate believed himself, a great fool and a great criminal. He should have cut himself adrift from society, and yet not be without society. He should have given up all, even Christ himself, for Christ's sake. He should be above fear or love or hate, and yet know them extremely well.

The same might be said of the saint; indeed, a wise man once said of some one that he was born too good ever to be a saint. According to Butler, it is only through our faults that we get experience and the wisdom and virtue that come of it; yet we must know that they

are faults before we can profit by them.
Nothing is so incapacitating as self-love; and
most of his ridicule was really directed against
that and against the idols begotten of it. "I
am the *enfant terrible* of literature and science,"
he says. "If I cannot, and I know I cannot,
get the literary and scientific big-wigs to give
me a shilling, I can, and I know I can, heave
bricks into the middle of them." He enjoyed
heaving bricks disinterestedly; but he took
good aim with them. It was one of his foibles
not to be impressed by reputations, however
great or old; for reputations are only dogmas,
and he was against all dogmas. So far as he
was concerned the most famous poet, painter,
or musician had to win his reputation, not to
impose it; and the Greek tragedians, Michelangelo, Bach, and Beethoven could win no
praise from him.

In all his judgments he was a typical insular
eccentric; indeed, he was the latest, and
perhaps the last, of that great race of eccentric
amateurs who are the glory and scandal of
England. A Frenchman or German of culture
would think him a mere barbarian to-day;
fifty years hence, perhaps, some German will
write a huge book about him, proving that he
was the father of modern thought, the great

rebel against romantic illusions, compared with whom Nietzsche was a rhetorician. Butler often talks like Nietzsche, as where he disputes Matthew Arnold's notion that "righteousness was to the Jew what strength and beauty were to the Greek or fortitude to the Roman."

This sounds well [he says] but can we think that the Jews, taken as a nation, were really more righteous than the Greeks and Romans? Could they indeed be so if they were less strong, graceful, and enduring?

And yet we are sure that he would not have liked Nietzsche, for Nietzsche was too much of a professional rebel and brow-beater for his taste. Nietzsche wrote as if he were a politician addressing a meeting of his own supporters; he flattered the self-love of other rebels, and encouraged them to think of themselves as a sect in possession of the truth. But Butler had no desire to form a sect or to address an audience of rebels.

But you, nice People! [he cries]
Who will be sick of me because the critics thrust
    me down your throats,
But who would take me willingly enough if you
    were not bored about me, . . .
Please remember that, if I were living, I should be
    upon your side

And should hate those who imposed me either on
    myself or others ;
Therefore, I pray you, neglect me, burlesque me,
    boil me down, do whatever you like with me,
But do not think that, if I were living, I should
    not aid and abet you.
There is nothing that even Shakespeare would
    enjoy more than a good burlesque of Hamlet.

And nothing, we may add, that Butler enjoyed
more than a good burlesque of human life,
which would amuse the nice people and shock
the professionals. The nice people were his
chosen audience, the people who have their
own likes and dislikes and are not committed
to any kind of theory ; the people who do not
want to impose themselves on others, and who
do not pretend to know or feel more than
they do know and feel. But that unassuming
word " nice " meant much when he used it ;
and, having said that a man was nice, he was
likely the next moment to say that he was saved.
This meant, finally, that he was disinterested,
not merely according to rule and in the ordinary
conduct of life, but in his very nature, seeking
no reward for his virtue even from his own
conscience, and being, indeed, unconscious of
it. Now and again in these notes Butler betrays his own passion for disinterestedness.

The world admits [he says] that there is

another world, that there is a kingdom, veritable and worth having, which, nevertheless, is invisible and has nothing to do with any kingdom such as we now see. It agrees that the wisdom of this other kingdom is foolishness here on earth, while the wisdom of the world is foolishness in the Kingdom of Heaven. In our hearts we know that the Kingdom of Heaven is the higher of the two and the better worth living and dying for, and that, if it is to be won, it must be sought steadfastly and in singleness of heart by those who put all else on one side and, shrinking from no sacrifice, are ready to face shame, poverty, and torture here rather than abandon the hope of the prize of their high calling. Nobody who doubts any of this is worth talking with.

And in answer to the question, How are we to find the Kingdom of Heaven? he says: "We are not likely to go wrong if in all simplicity, humility, and good faith we heartily desire to find it and follow the dictates of ordinary common sense."

Butler believed and insisted that common sense was necessary to salvation, was, indeed, a symptom of it. That was where he differed from Romantics and from the worldly alike. Romantics think common sense is no concern of theirs, and the worldly think it is only their concern. Butler set it above the scorn of the one class and the patronage of the other. It was a gift, he held, to be cultivated for all purposes, and as necessary to the saint and the artist as to the man of business; the fact that they pursue different ends makes no difference. Life is a matter of execution as well as of conception; and if the execution is poor it will pervert the conception. His sharpest satire was directed against the people who pervert their conception with bad execution—the sentimentalists, doctrinaires, Pharisees; all the people who love themselves and their own theories better than anything else, and who therefore never test their theories by results. In all this Butler, however much he may like to shock us in detail, follows the great orthodox tradition of the ages. He is with Socrates against the Sophists and with Christ against the Pharisees. "Forget yourself and love others," he says, "and you shall attain to common sense and be one of the nice people— in fact, you shall be saved." He puts it all prosaically because in our time the worldly have captured prose as the Romantics have captured poetry; and it was his aim to deliver prose, like common sense, from the clutches of the worldly. If he had been a poet he would no doubt have tried to deliver poetry from the clutches of the Romantics. As it was he wrote one piece, the In Memoriam to H.R.F., which is poetry in its matter and half-poetry in its form; and no one knows Butler who has not read this. But no one knows him who has not read this book through; and perhaps it will come to be the most read and valued of all his books.

The Life of Samuel Butler 〜 〜

SAMUEL BUTLER often spoke against
the sin of biographers, which is greater
than they know. By refusing to tell the
whole truth, or the most interesting part of it,
not only do they make their biographies dull,
but they mislead and discourage mankind.
The great man, as they present him, has
attained to a perfection both impossible and
insipid; we despair of being like him and do
not wish to be like him; we may think him a
Parsifal, but we resent him as a pure fool.
Butler himself said of his Life of his grand-
father, Dr. Butler:—

It is better that I should be indiscreet and
dishonourable than that men's true minds
should be concealed and turned again to false-
hood, if we have a chance of getting at them.
It is next to never that we can get at any
man's genuine opinion on any subject, except
the weather or eating and drinking; and when
we can do so directly or indirectly neither

The Life of Samuel Butler

amour propre nor discretion should be allowed to veil it, for there is nothing in this world so precious nor is there any other stuff from which genuine fresh opinion can derive.

Mr. Festing Jones, who, like Butler himself, has a gift for humanizing the wisdom of the serpent, is careful to quote this in the preface to his Life of Butler; it is his answer to those who may accuse him of indiscretion. He has written as if for Butler to read; and we are sure that, whatever anyone else thinks about the book, Butler would have liked it. His method is the method of Boswell; he seems to tell all he knows, but his interest in his subject has made him select by instinct what is interesting because it describes Butler. The book in form is a chronicle, all narrative and little description; but the narrative describes, and, with each chapter, we know more of Butler, as a man living and changing and growing before us; we cannot know him completely until we have read to the end, because he himself was completed only by death. In fact, it is one of the best biographies in the language, a document of human nature, because it shows us a particular man in all his circumstances of time and place, and a document which, as we read it, we know we can trust.

Butler liked to present himself in his books as a smiling invulnerable critic of the universe; but here we learn how often he was wounded. He might, if he had chosen, have made a tragedy of *The Way of All Flesh*; but he would not exhibit the pageant of his bleeding heart, because he wished it to bleed as little as possible. As we read, we discover that life was not kind to him, and that he was always trying to armour himself against fate. To begin with, his childhood was unhappy; in a letter written when he was forty, he says, " I have had the worst three years I ever had since the horrors of childhood and boyhood"; and he did not often complain of anything. Then for many years he mistook his vocation, trying to paint when he was born to write; he lost a great part of his money through trusting in friends; he found after many years that he had wasted affection on his dearest male friend; and, what was almost worse, his dearest female friend seemed to be wasting her affection on him, at least he believed that she wished to be his wife, while he did not wish to be her husband. So there was a misfit both ways; and he remained a bachelor, hungry for a happiness which he knew to exist.

The Life of Samuel Butler

That is one side of him, concealed in his public writings, but now revealed without undue emphasis in Mr. Jones's narrative. One might have guessed it from *Erewhon Revisited*, which is made beautiful and moving by the hero's hunger for affection, Butler's own hunger, for he always wrote autobiography in his stories, and cared for nothing in other stories that was not autobiography. He was a disappointed man, and his disappointments made him suspicious; hence his grievance against Darwin. As Mr. Jones says, with an affection too great not to be candid, "Butler felt he had been taken in. It was John Picard Owen and the chickens over again; it was the alleged death and resurrection of Jesus Christ over again; it was his own education over again; and there was nothing for it but to investigate the whole subject and write a book about it. This book was *Evolution, Old and New*." Butler, with his attacks now on religion, now on science, is to be understood only when we see him in process of finding out the world. There was a conspiracy to keep him, young, unsuspecting, and generous, in the dark, to exploit his best qualities and the best qualities of all the young. His father tried to make a parson of him by concealing the facts about the Gospels, and his father was only a party to one great conspiracy. Darwin tried to make him believe that there was no intelligence in the order of the universe by concealing the facts about the universe; and he was only a party to another great conspiracy. So finally he revenged himself on his father in *The Way of all Flesh* and *The Fair Haven*; and on Darwin in a series of books; but he was always trying to purge himself of the bitterness which these deceptions provoked in him: he would not be a weakling squealing against his oppressors; if he was deceived it was his own fault. It is more immoral, he insisted, to be prey than a beast of prey; he would be neither, but a man who explained to the beast of prey the very processes by which, unconsciously, he hypnotized his victims. He disliked his father not so much for being a serpent as for persuading himself that he was a dove; he saw the world infested with serpents disguised, even to themselves, as doves, and so lacking the beauty of the serpent; and his mission, or his pleasure, was to undisguise these prudish serpents, to the world and to themselves.

Butler tried to be fair to his father. In 1883 he wrote this note on their relations :—

He never liked me, nor I him; from my

146

earliest recollections I can call to mind no
time when I did not fear him and dislike him;
over and over again I have relented towards
him and said to myself that he was a good
fellow after all; but I had hardly done so
when he would go for me in some way or other
which soured me again. I have no doubt I have
made myself very disagreeable; certainly I have
done many very silly and wrong things; I am
not at all sure that the fault is more his than
mine. But no matter whose it is, the fact
remains that for years and years I have never
passed a day without thinking of him many
times over as the man who was sure to be
against me, and who would see the bad side
rather than the good of everything I said and
did.

It would be futile now to judge either of them;
but the story of their enmity has value because
it shows us how grudges often grow up between
father and son, and how they may be prevented.
In this case the father never understood the
workings of his own mind; he had been trained
to conceal them from himself, never to admit
to himself that he did anything because he
wished to do it. The son saw his motives
with fatal clearness and despised him for
refusing to see them; the father was afraid of
him without knowing that he was afraid, or
why; and his fear, driven like all his real feel-

ings into his unconscious mind, disguised itself
as dislike and disapproval. Butler, who could
not speak frankly to his father on any subject,
because of the convention established in the
family that the father could do no wrong,
spoke frankly of his father in his own mind
and in *The Way of all Flesh*, but did not so
purge himself of bitterness. He still kept his
opinion, and his art, a secret from his father,
and there remained, on the one side this secret,
on the other unconscious fear because of it; on
the one side satire, on the other moral disapproval, as weapons in a warfare always
suppressed and so never ended. The moral,
for parents, is that, if they do not know themselves, their children will know them.

But Butler's worst enemy was his closest
friend. The story of Charles Paine Pauli is
stranger than fiction, and would be incredible
if it had not happened. Butler got to know
him in New Zealand, and admired him as being
all that he himself was not: handsome, attractive, a man of the world who knew where to
get well-fitting clothes and how to wear them.
But Pauli had no money and was in bad health;
Butler believed that, if he stayed in New Zealand,
he would die. So they both returned to England,
Butler lending him £100 for the voyage and

promising to pay him £200 a year for three years so that he might be called to the Bar. This was in 1864, and Butler continued to support Pauli, as he supposed, until Pauli's death in 1897. Pauli never would tell him anything about his affairs; and for some time Butler lived in penury, sharing what he had with Pauli. Their friendship was not happy; Butler thought that Pauli was possessed by a dumb devil. "The wrongness of his silence wounded me. I told him that I thought it wrong, but he said he would tell me if he could—it was so difficult to say exactly what he was earning—people did not pay him, etc., and I, still believing him to be much as I was myself in the matter of good faith, accepted his excuses." Even when Butler lost nearly all his money, Pauli would not tell him anything of his private affairs, nor where he lived, nor whether he was making anything at the Bar; and they never met except when Pauli came over from Lincoln's Inn to lunch at Butler's early dinner in Clifford's Inn. But still Butler tried to believe the best of Pauli; said he was kind to animals, and behaved with all the infatuation of a bachelor who, unconsciously, tries to make a friend the substitute for a wife. In 1897 Pauli died without sending for Butler, who saw his death in *The Times*. He then discovered that Pauli had at one time earned from £800 to £900 a year at the Bar, but lately only about £500. He left £9000, none of it to Butler; and he had been receiving money from other friends. Butler wrote a full account of his relations with Pauli, and said at the end of it: "My main feeling is one of thankfulness that I never suspected the facts. . . . The only decent end for such a white heat of devotion as mine was to him for so many years was the death of one or other of the parties concerned. . . . I felt pretty sure I was doing a great deal too much, but I would rather have done a great deal too much than a little too little." In 1901 he wrote this note: "I knew I was being cruelly treated, but how cruelly I never knew till after his death, when I could not even forgive him, as I would have done."

The great satirists are always men who, one way or another, have been cruelly injured; their love is negative in their art because it has been baulked; but we can see how much Butler was injured in the affair of Pauli from the fact that he, who made so much of his art out of autobiography, could never use this story for satire; he could only write a plain account of it. We can see also that he tried to make himself out a kind of Sancho Panza to all the false quixotries of the world because he was really a Don Quixote. It was a case of protective mimicry, in which the fly managed to persuade himself, and the wasps, that he had a sharper sting than theirs.

It is interesting to know that he drew Towneley in *The Way of all Flesh* from Pauli. It was not a good likeness, for it expressed only his illusions about Pauli and also about the Towneleys of the world, whom he admired just because he did not understand them. The man who quite simply and brutally exploits others, who takes without giving always, was different in kind from Butler; and Butler, who suffered from his own passion for giving, admired him as an artist admires a Bengal tiger, admired him as a perfect and finished product, while he himself had the malease, the unpreparedness, the inadequacy, of incessant growth. This in his satire he tried to conceal; there he consoled himself by pretending to be a pure ironic mind; but, far more truly than Byron, he smiled so that he might not weep, or so that his tears might not be seen.

His quarrel with Darwin was irrational

151

enough—so irrational that we must look for the cause of it behind the actual facts; and the cause was his own *odium theologicum*. He was angry with Darwin and all his followers because he thought they denied intelligence to the universe, and still more because they denied love to it. They emptied all things of value; and he cared ultimately for nothing but the values of man. He cared for them so much that he would not have them too easily justified—to sentimentalize the universe was almost worse than to make it out full of sound and fury signifying nothing. As he himself said, he was always ready to give up Christ for Christ's sake; but the most real things in the universe to him were the Christian virtues, and he was not content to leave them hanging in a meaningless void. " There is a something as yet but darkly known which makes right right and wrong wrong." He was angry with the men of science because, as it seemed to him, they were trying to prove, even when they were not sharp enough to see it themselves, that there is nothing which makes right right and wrong wrong. Hence his attitude to the Church, which will surprise many readers of this book. In 1880 he wrote to the Bishop of Carlisle :—

152

The Life of Samuel Butler

If those who start with an all-pervading, supreme intelligence can yet find nothing out of harmony with their initial assumption in a theory of evolution, which is attended at each step by mind, purpose, and the exercise of the moral qualities ; and if, again, those who, like myself, start with *tabulæ rasæ*, and, working up from the first thing they can lay hold of, find themselves driven first to evolution, then to purposive evolution, and through this to the action of a supreme, all-pervading mind or purpose in both organic and inorganic matter ; then surely we may be upon the eve of the removal of other misunderstandings.

Two years later he wrote: "It is not the Bishops and Archbishops I am afraid of. Men like Huxley and Tyndall are my natural enemies, and I am always glad when I find church people recognizing that the differences between them and me are, as I believe myself, more of words than things." You may almost say that he chastened the Church because he loved it; but he did not love the men of science. You could be on your guard against the Church, and its exasperating habit of telling little lies in the cause of a great truth ; but the men of science, he thought, told little truths in the cause of a great lie; and the world was not on its guard against them.

They had deceived even him; and a burnt
child, if it is Butler, hates the fire.

I insist upon this side of Butler's experience
and character because it will be new to most
readers; but Mr. Jones does not insist upon
it; he lets it appear in the course of his
narrative. Butler suffered much in life, but
he was not unhappy; he wrestled with life,
conquered it, and enjoyed the sense of his own
victory. In 1898 he wrote: "If in my books
from *Erewhon* (1872) to *Luck or Cunning?*
(1887) there is a something behind the written
words which the reader can feel but not grasp
—and I fancy that this must be so—it is due,
I believe, to the sense of wrong which was
omnipresent with me, not only in regard to
Pauli, the Darwins, and my father, but also
in regard to my ever-present anxiety about
money." If that were the whole truth, if
Butler had been cradled into prose by wrong
and nothing else, his books would be dispirit-
ing, which they are not. There is something
else behind the written words which the reader
can feel; and that is the sense of victory, even
before it was won. Butler always believed in
victory, to be won not so much by an heroic
defiance of men and things, as by smiling both
at and with them. If there was a practical

joke in the universe, he would rob it of its
sting by seeing the point of it; and he did
not believe that the joke was really a cruel
one. There was nothing he believed in so
much as kindness; and he thought one could
win it, even from the nature of things, by
refusing to be frightened into unkindness.
So, by taste and on principle, he was the
kindest of men and won happiness that way.
There was nothing he enjoyed more than
his relations with his servant Alfred; they
were to him a symbol of his success in life;
and we can see what they were from a letter
which Alfred wrote him in 1891 :—

DEAR SIR,—I hope you arrived quite safe
on Tuesday and found your sister well. . . . I
have a little complaint to make. You never
looked out of the carriage to see me standing
on the platform as I always do. There was I
standing in the rain and you never looked at
me. . . .—Yours truly, ALFRED.

On receiving this, Butler sent an apology by
telegram, and Alfred replied :—

Received telegram this morning, thank you.
I showed it to Mr. Jones and he laughed. I
forgive you.—ALFRED.

If bitterness had overcome Butler, he would
have known that life had beaten him; as it

was—out of the strong came forth sweetness, though with a quick, peculiar flavour of its own. There are many likenesses of him, including portraits by himself; but the one which is most like the Butler of this book is a photograph taken by Alfred in 1898. It is a queer mixture of an anthropoid ape and a god, expressing exactly Butler's own view of evolution; the god is in the making, and would be a little bored if there were not still something of the monkey in him. Mr. Jones has not left the monkey out of his book any more than the god; it will increase both the gaiety and the faith of nations.

Turgenev ∽ ∽ ∽ ∽ ∽

WHEN you enjoy a writer thoroughly you do not ask yourself whether he is superior to some other writer, as, when you love anyone, you do not ask whether he is better than some one else. It is when we have passed out of the fresh enjoyment of an artist that we become his partisans. Mr. Edward Garnett, unfortunately, begins his Study of Turgenev as a partisan. His first chapter is on Turgenev's critics and detractors. He starts in a bad temper because there are those who think Tolstoy and Dostoevsky greater. This heresy, he tells us, arose in Russia; and he will have it that anyone in England who shares it is imitating some Russian. Mr. Maurice Baring " has echoed various Russian critics," he is not to be credited with an opinion of his own. And Mr. Conrad in his Foreword is also angry with those who prefer Dostoevsky. " You know very well, my dear Edward, that if you had Antinous himself in a booth of the world's fair, and killed yourself in protesting that his soul was as perfect as his body, you wouldn't get one per cent. of the crowd struggling next door for a sight of the double-headed nightingale or of some weak-kneed giant grinning through a horse collar." Thus it is that Mr. Conrad expresses his own preference for Turgenev. We did not know until we read Mr. Garnett's book that there was this prevailing depreciation of Turgenev; but Mr. Garnett tells us all about it, and works himself into a rage over it, just as if he were an antivivisectionist or a Baconian. S o, if you have read Turgenev innocently and enjoyed him as you should, you will probably hurry past this first chapter on critics and detractors to discover what Mr. Garnett has to say when he has recovered from his anger at those who do not think Turgenev the greatest of Russian novelists. For, after all, what does it matter if A and B prefer Dostoevsky to Turgenev, and say so? Life is too short for these literary feuds, at least if you care for literature.

Unfortunately, Mr. Garnett never escapes from his partisanship. Throughout the book he has his eye on Turgenev's position rather than on Turgenev himself. He is always protesting that he is a perfect Antinous; and this is a pity, for when he does forget to worship his idol he says good things about him and his characters, as that his Tatyana in *Smoke* "is born to corrupt, but never to be corrupted." We wish that he had not been so much the slave of his enthusiasm; for Turgenev is now far enough away from us both in time and in fashion to be treated justly. But for Mr. Garnett he is still a neglected contemporary; and he writes always as if he must shake us out of our ignorance and prejudice. So, much of his book seems to belong to the past; we are not conscious of any prejudice against Turgenev, and we do not care to be scolded for it.

Yet, perhaps, the world has grown colder to him than it should be, and it is worth while to inquire the reason of this. We have always wondered, for instance, why Tolstoy was so much irritated by him. Mr. Garnett speaks of his "lifelong hostility to Turgenev's genius, only removed by the latter's death." That seems to suggest envy, which is certainly not the explanation. Perhaps Turgenev was too much of an artist for Tolstoy, too much specialized; for there was nothing Tolstoy hated so much as specialization. His book, *What is Art?*, is one long attack on the specialization of the artist. To Tolstoy and to

Dostoevsky writing was a natural process, like talking; but to Turgenev it was more of a ritual, as to Flaubert. He wrote, or seemed to write, with an exquisite naturalness; he was far too well bred to be shoppy in anything; but he looked at life like an artist, like one who was going to make use of it. Tolstoy lived it; and his writing was only an extra consciousness, an effort to live yet more intensely in words than in actual fact. He is like a man who sings at his work; whereas Turgenev is like a man playing an instrument, a very big man playing a very small instrument. After reading *A House of Gentlefolk* or *Fathers and Children*, one is filled with the sense of great power producing a very small and exquisite sound. Tolstoy's books are full almost to confusion. Turgenev's are exquisitely empty like a Japanese room. It is not a barren emptiness, but the result of an austere inhibition; everything in it is typical, and he admits no detail irrelevant to the type. His characters never run away with him, or with themselves.

What passion, what knowledge, what obstinate questioning is implied in Bazarov, the hero of *Fathers and Children*! But it is all implied. Turgenev will not speak out about it. All the Russian novelists are

distant to their readers compared with the
English, compared with Dickens or Charlotte
Brontë. They tell us more, but they do not
confide; they seem to speak to a general
abstract public, and not to the particular
reader. But Turgenev is the most distant of
them all; he writes almost like a philosopher,
as if he would disdain to convince us of anything by a personal appeal. So Bazarov is
like a thesis come to life. He is utterly convincing while we read; but he is not quite
human, like Levin or Myshkin, because he
always speaks and acts in character. He lacks
the richness, the irrelevance, of reality, that
last illusion which a writer can produce only
when his characters produce it on him, when
he has forgotten his design in them. Turgenev never does that; but it is not because
of the æsthetic poverty of his mind. We
may be sure that he knew and perceived and
felt abundantly; all his observations are too
perfectly relevant, too easily precise, to have
been brought in because he wished to make
use of them. But in each case his mind was
possessed by the type; and he would not allow
the individual to trespass beyond it.

That, perhaps, was what irritated Tolstoy,
to whom men were utterly individual, and

for whom life was a fierce conflict between the individual and the laws of God. To Turgenev it was rather a conflict between the type and the laws of Nature. The anarchy of the world for Tolstoy is in man and in his disobedience to God. Why is man thus disobedient? That is the question he asks. For him all the sorrow and suffering of life come from man himself, from the individual sinner. But to Turgenev they come from man's incompatibility with Nature; and the question he asks is, Why is the universe what it is? In the last scene of *Fathers and Children*, where the dead Bazarov's old father cries, " I said I should rebel, I rebel! I rebel!" Turgenev, says Mr. Garnett, epitomizes in one stroke the infinite aspiration, the eternal insignificance, of the life of man. That is always the drama for him, a little group of human beings, aspiring and thwarted by a surrounding indifference. And for him there are two kinds of human beings: those who aspire and are thwarted, and those who basely comply with Nature and become themselves part of that which thwarts. Of Maria Nikolaevna, the woman who seduces the hero in *Torrents of Spring*, Mr. Garnett says that "in her ruthless charm she is the incarnation of a cruel principle in Nature."

Turgenev

But that is true of all the evil characters of
Turgenev, whether they are lustful like her
or merely worldly. They seem to be con-
spiring with Nature to bring the dreams of
his heroes and heroines to naught. They are
like the big, dull boy at school who bullies
and derides the weak and sensitive. For him
human stupidity is part of the stupidity of the
universe, and the few who rise above it are
crushed by it or by circumstance. And yet he
does passionately believe in those few and loves
them passionately; they are to him beautiful,
inexplicable flowers in a barren wilderness;
they make life worth living, and yet fill it
with pain. Like St. Paul, he cries that there
is nothing worth having but love, but to him
love is a beautiful, forlorn irrelevance in a world
unfitted for its survival. All his heroes fight a
losing battle, not merely with the fools of the
world, but with the nature of things. And so
all his beauty and tenderness seem to be but a
pathetic interlude, a strain of music suddenly
drowned by noise; and the point of the book
always is this sudden marring of the music.
At the end you are not thrilled and heartened
by the sense of escape; rather, you are cut off
suddenly from what you love, and made to feel
that this separation is for ever, is in the nature

of things. The mechanism of the universe closes in upon you; and it is mere mechanism. Those who consent to live like machines are the winners now and for ever.

Now one has only to state this attitude of Turgenev to see that it is not the modern attitude. We, whatever we believe, do not, like him, suffer from this sense of the treachery of things. There is to us more mystery than treachery in them; and we cannot, like him, divide human beings into sheep and goats, into those who basely consent to Nature and those who are piteously crushed by her. To us, as to Tolstoy, human stupidity is unnatural rather than natural; it is rebellion rather than compliance. In fact, as a thinker, Turgenev is old-fashioned. That "sad philosophy" of his which Mr. Garnett finds implied in the ending of *A House of Gentlefolk* is to us no philosophy at all, but merely the cry of one who has been hurt by life; and all his books are cries of pain, though the cries of one who knows how to make them beautiful.

In his last illness he said: "When my sufferings are unendurable, I follow Schopenhauer's advice. I analyse my sensations and my agony departs for a period." In all his books he seems to be doing that, and with the

same sad purpose; he is an artist so that he
may not suffer too much from life by losing
himself in it. Thus to him his art is more
than life itself. If he could, he would be
utterly a spectator; but he was too great a man,
too much of a lover, for that. So for him there
is in all the affections more pathos than joy;
for they are what tie us to life; they give us
the dream of happiness, and yet make it impossible. He sings St. Paul's Hymn to Love
in a very minor key; and it is to him not love
triumphant, but love the betrayer and the
betrayed.

So perhaps Mr. Garnett is right after all,
and we are unjust to him. We cannot understand what he is so sorrowful about. He
belongs to the past of the Romantics who con-
sented utterly to their griefs. To the modern
mind sorrow is something to be conquered, or
to be laughed away as a little unreal. It is a
proof of failure rather than of any kind of
success; or at best it is a phase from which we
hope and try to escape. But Turgenev settles
down in it, not with any gross luxury of woe,
but as if it were the business of man to make
pain tolerable by analysing it, as if the pleasure
of analysis were some by-product of human life
which man, in the universal unreason of things,

may utilize, as we utilize coal-tar in our drugs. But we cannot now consent to believe in the universal unreason; and so Turgenev's art, with all its beauty, seems to us pathological, and, as we read, we ask, What was the matter with him?

But that is a foolish attitude; for in all great writers it is the product that matters and not the process. So we feel some sympathy, after all, with Mr. Garnett's anger. What irritates him is our want of sympathy; and it irritates him the more because he still shares Turgenev's view of life, and is therefore able to enjoy him like a contemporary. That cry— "I rebel! I rebel!"—is to him not the cry of a period, not the expression of a type, but the natural everlasting cry of humanity. He also rebels; and to him Turgenev is the expression of himself. He says Yes to Turgenev's version of life; but most of us now say No to it, as Tolstoy did. It is not that life seems to us more pleasant than he made it, but that it means more. Yet it is foolish to be hindered by this intellectual difference from the æsthetic enjoyment of him. He may have been wrong intellectually, and in his comment upon life; but that is a matter of argument. The beauty of his work is not a matter of argument. But

Turgenev

we can see it only if we sympathize with him, if we see him as a wonderful and beautiful human being, who suffered more than most men, and whose books express his suffering in terms of beauty. And it is easy to sympathize with him, because sympathy is the secret of his own excellence. It is a limited sympathy, for he does divide men and women very sharply into sheep and goats; he is afraid of the stupid, as he is afraid of Nature, and his fear expresses itself in cold dislike. But for the innocent, the passionate, the pure in heart, for all those who are blest in the Sermon on the Mount, he has a tenderness that makes music of his words and of his very plot. Protest, if you will, that life is not like this; yet you must admit that life itself has drawn this music out of a beautiful mind. Turgenev's novels are nearer to poetry than any others, because his comment on life is so purely emotional. Like Schubert, he makes his songs out of sorrow; all his exquisite precision of detail, all his skill of construction, are means of expressing that. His very characters are mouthpieces of it, and subdued to its minor key. So his books have the unity of music; and, if Mr. Garnett chooses to value this unity above all other qualities of art, he has a right

to do so. I began his book with some irrita-
tion, because he was irritated. I ended it with
sympathy, both for him and for Turgenev.
Therefore he has, after all, produced on me the
effect which, no doubt, he wished to produce.

The Clash of East and West in Thought

MR. STEPHEN GRAHAM tells us that all that is positive in modern Russian thought springs from the teaching of Solovyof. Introducing his book, *The Justification of the Good*, he says: "Tolstoy we know; Dostoevsky we know; and now comes a new force into our life, Solovyof, the greatest of the three." Certainly *The Justification of the Good* is worth reading, but not because Solovyof is greater than Tolstoy or Dostoevsky. They remade the novel, but he has not remade moral philosophy; indeed, he has failed in that which he set out to do—namely, to justify the good; and he has failed because the good is not entirely good to him. There is in his mind a conflict between a natural Oriental pessimism and an acquired Western optimism; and this conflict makes the weakness, and the interest, of his book. He himself is entirely unaware of it; to himself he is a Christian; but his Christianity is tainted by ancient heresies natural to the Eastern mind, and so natural to him that he thinks they are a part of Christianity. In actual Christianity there always has been a drift towards Manicheism, checked again and again by conscious dogmatic statement or unconscious revolt. The very affirmation that God made all things in heaven and earth is a denial of Manicheism; but here we find it still possessing the mind of a trained philosopher just as it possessed the mind of Tolstoy. Again it comes to us out of the East, a dark, Asiatic madness, a melancholy deeper than thought, betraying itself in Solovyof's very conception of the nature of morality. He protests, as we have said, that he is a Christian, and denounces Schopenhauer; yet, wherever he is a Christian, he is inconsistent with his own first principles. In them he is a follower of Schopenhauer, or rather one of those Eastern pessimists whom Schopenhauer followed with a European zest that denied his own pessimism. Schopenhauer was consistent in thought, but his mood, his cheerful malice, contradicted his thought; Solovyof is inconsistent in thought, but underlying that inconsistency there is a mood of despondency which betrays itself whenever he speaks with most conviction.

Clash of East and West in Thought

He professes to be an advocate of the universe; but his heart is not in the work, and he fails to make the universe seem attractive. That is the mark of the true pessimist; try as he will, he cannot make us like his version of the universe; the more he praises it, the more we rebel. At best he can only preach contentment, and we cannot be content to be content with the universe; we must finally side with exultation or with despair.

Solovyof's pessimism betrays itself at once in his account of "the primary data of morality." According to him, "the fundamental feelings of shame, pity, and reverence exhaust the sphere of man's possible moral relations to that which is below him, that which is on a level with him, that which is above him." Pity, for him, is the origin of love and is itself a more moral feeling than love. He believes that, because he believes that all good has its origin in pain; he is unable to conceive of a good state of mind that is not painful to him who experiences it. "Love in itself," he says, "or love in general, is not a virtue; the virtue behind it, the unconditioned virtue, is always pity." But this is contrary to the Christian faith, and contrary also, we believe, to all human ex-

perience. Solovyof's very psychology is perverted by his pessimism; of the mother,
whether human or animal, he says that no
mental state but pity "can express her original
solidarity with her weak, helpless, piteous off-
spring wholly dependent upon her." But,
according both to the Christian faith and to
experience, a mother's love is deeper than pity;
pity is only an incident of it. Solovyof would
persuade us that love, like all good things, is
necessarily painful in its origin; it comes of
suffering the pains and sorrows of others, and
its joy is but the result of that suffering. But,
according to the Christian faith, love is deeper
than both joy and sorrow — these are but
incidents of it which it accepts and to which
it gives a quality, a meaning, they lack without
it. And, as a fact, the mother, human or
animal, is not always pitying her piteous off-
spring. The cat, the best of mothers, delights
in her kittens, which are far from always piteous.
The natural tie between her and them, the tie
between any mother and her child, is not pity,
it is motherhood and childhood, which means
love.

But Solovyof, in denying that love is a
virtue, betrays the fact that, in his profound
pessimism, he does not know the meaning of

the word love. "Selfish love for oneself and
one's property, passionate love of drink or of
horse racing, is not reckoned as a virtue." But
these are not love. Men cannot love themselves; self-love is only a metaphor, a *reductio
ad absurdum* of egotism. It means that the
egotist is so incapable of love that he would
love himself if he could. Self-love is a word
for a negative, meaning the absence of love for
others; and when we speak of the love of
property or drink, we also use the word meta-
phorically; we mean that a man commits the
absurdity of behaving as if it were possible to
love these things. Solovyof quotes the words
of St. John—"Love not the world"—which,
he says, are an expression of the fundamental
principle of asceticism. But asceticism itself
is not fundamental, except for pessimists like
Solovyof. It is a negative means to a positive
end, a means to love. When we say that a
man loves the world, or anything else that
cannot be an object of love, we mean that he
is, by some kind of egotism, preventing himself
from loving. Love is self-forgetfulness in
something that can be loved, but Solovyof does
not really believe in the existence of that which
can be loved for its own sake. He tries, but
unconsciously, instinctively, he fails. Still he

says that love of our neighbour has its source in pity, and love of God in reverence, which means to him fear or gratitude. He is too despondent to affirm in either that quality which directly moves us to love. The great positive passion does not exist for him because to him the universe, God Himself, is negative, forbidding; and all good consists in refusing and in the pain of refusal. Thus he says, in a curious passage, that to share another's joys is not so good in itself as to share his sorrows.

Participation in the pleasures of others may always have an element of self-interest. Even in the case of an old man sharing the joy of a child doubt may be felt with regard to the altruistic nature of the sentiment; for in any case it is pleasant for the old man to refresh the memory of his own happy childhood. On the contrary, all genuine feeling of regret at the suffering of others, whether moral or physical, is painful for the person who experiences that feeling, and is therefore opposed to his egotism. This is clear from the fact that sincere grief about others disturbs our personal joy, damps our mirth, that is, proves to be incompatible with the state of selfish satisfaction.

One could not imply more clearly that God does not wish us to be happy, that He has made a universe in which we can be good only through suffering. But the Christian doctrine

of love asserts that he who loves will consent
to both the joys and the sorrows of love, that
love itself is good, not joy or sorrow.

> Joy and grief are woven fine,
> A garment for the soul divine.
> And when this we truly know,
> Safely through the world we go.

A state of mind is not good because it is
painful; the joy we take in the joys of others
is not egotistical because it is joy; indeed,
the egotist is prevented by his egotism from
feeling it. The good state of mind is love;
and it is to be valued because it is love, whether
it brings us joy or sorrow. Solovyof confuses
pleasure with joy; participation in the pleasures
of others will have an element of self-interest,
if it is not the result of love but of the desire
to share the pleasures. But love cannot come
of the desire to share pleasures, although it
alone enables us to share both joy and sorrow.
Here, as elsewhere, the psychology of Solovyof
is wrong, because, for him, the universe forbids.

But it is when he comes to speak of shame
and the sexual instinct that his Manichean
madness most clearly betrays itself. Conscience, he says, is simply the development of
shame. "The whole moral life of man, in all
its three aspects, springs from a root that is

distinctly human and essentially foreign to the animal world." But shame is a negative feeling, it is dislike, it says, Do not; and if conscience, if our whole moral life, springs from this negative origin, it loses value for us the moment we are aware of the fact. We cannot consent to a universe in which that is so. Imputing this source to the good, Solovyof at once fails to justify it for us; the Kingdom of Heaven itself is for him a negative, to which we attain by being ashamed, not of "this world," but of our very selves. True, he says that "the object of condemnation in asceticism is not material nature as such. From no point of view can it be rationally maintained that nature considered objectively —whether in its essence or in its appearances— is evil." But here it is only the acquired Western part of him that speaks, and it is contradicted in a few pages by the instinctive Oriental. He says that the animal life in man must be subordinate to the spiritual; but he means that it must be denied and destroyed by the spiritual.

The moral question with regard to the sexual function is in the first place the question of one's inner relation to it, of passing judgment upon it as such. How are we inwardly to regard this fact from the point of view of the final norm, of the absolute good—are we to approve of it or to condemn it . . . to affirm and develop or to deny, limit, and finally to abolish it?

Solovyof says we are to abolish it.

The carnal means of production is for man an evil . . . our moral relation to this fact must be absolutely negative. We must adopt the path that leads to its limitation and abolition; how and when it will be abolished in humanity as a whole or even in ourselves is a question that has nothing to do with Ethics.

Here is the very doctrine of the *Kreutzer Sonata;* but in Solovyof it is supported by a dark mysticism which he never clearly expresses. According to him the carnal means of production is somehow the cause of death. "Man's final acceptance of the kingdom of death, which is maintained and perpetuated by carnal reproduction, deserves absolute condemnation." Such, he says, is "the positive Christian point of view, which decides this all-important question according to the spirit and not according to the letter and, consequently, without any external exclusiveness." True, the Manichean drift of Christianity has always existed; but always Christianity has resisted

M　　177

it, always its bright positive has overcome that dark negative; and even Solovyof allows a practical compromise with his own doctrine, though the doctrine itself he insists is true, in the following curious passage:—

The idea that the preaching of sexual abstinence, however energetic and successful, may prematurely stop the propagation of the human race and lead to its annihilation is so absurd that one may justly doubt the sincerity of those who hold it. It is not likely that anyone can seriously fear this particular danger for humanity. So long as the change of generations is necessary for the development of the human kind, the taste for bringing that change about will certainly not disappear in men.

He does not see that, if the change of generations is necessary for the development of the human kind, it is the darkest pessimism, implying the malignity of God Himself, to hold that the process necessary for that change is itself sinful.

But Solovyof, as soon as he comes to deal with economics, escapes from his own madness, and indeed supplies an antidote to it. Here he is subject to Western thought, here he is no longer a pessimist or a Manichee, and here he escapes from his psychological error. In the chapter on the Economic Question, he insists that man is not entirely an economic being, that the economic man is a figment of bad metaphysics; and he points out, very shrewdly, that Marxian Socialism has been infected with the error of the "bourgeois" economics which it set out to destroy.

The defect of the orthodox school of political economy—the Liberal, or more exactly the Anarchical, school—is that it separates on principle the economic sphere from the moral. The defect of Socialism is that it more or less confuses or wrongly identifies these two distinct, though indivisible, spheres. From the plutocratic point of view the normal man is, in the first place, a capitalist, and then, *per accidens*, a citizen, head of a family, an educated man, member of some religious union, etc. Similarly, from the Socialist point of view all other interests become insignificant and retreat into the background—if they do not disappear altogether before the economic interest.

In fact, the error of the economic maniacs is of the same nature as the error of the sex-maniacs. Both find but one content in human nature, whether it be sex or the struggle for life; and Marxian Socialism is based upon that monomania, like plutocracy. Both, says

Solovyof, have the same motto—"Man liveth by bread alone." "The struggle between the two hostile camps is not one of principle. . . . One party is concerned with the material welfare of the capitalist minority, the other with the material welfare of the labour majority." It could not be better put, though it is not true of all kinds of Socialism; and in refuting it Solovyof also refutes his own Manicheism. "Economic relations," he says,

are based upon a simple and ultimate fact, which cannot, as such, be deduced from the moral principle—the fact, namely, that work, labour, is necessary to the maintenance of life. . . . The necessity to work in order to obtain the means of livelihood is, indeed, a matter of fate and independent of human will. But it is merely an impetus which spurs men to activity, the further course of that activity being determined by psychological and moral, not by economic, causes.

And, again, "productive labour, possession and enjoyment of its results, is one of the aspects of human life or one of the spheres of human activity." Now apply all this admirable doctrine to "carnal reproduction." It also is a simple and ultimate fact, which cannot be deduced, as such, from the moral principle. It also is necessary to the maintenance of human life; and the fact that it is so is independent of the human will. To say that it is evil in itself is as if one said that the instinct of self-preservation was evil in itself; which is to condemn the nature of the universe, as we know it. Solovyof, when he comes to economics, does not condemn the nature of the universe or of man, because economics is a wholly Western study and he has not read his own Eastern heresy into it. But, inevitably, if he had thought consistently he would have been forced either by his economic doctrine to give up his Manicheism, or by his Manicheism to give up his economic doctrine. The two are incompatible, but Solovyof did not discover it. So the interest of his book is not in its philosophy, but in that conflict between East and West which divides it into two inconsistent parts. The very sincerity of the writer makes the conflict the more patent. Here we have in philosophical terms the tragedy of Tolstoy's last years; for Manicheism makes life impossible; and that is why Christianity, which says that life is not only possible but glorious, must always condemn it.